the library and information
professional's internet companion

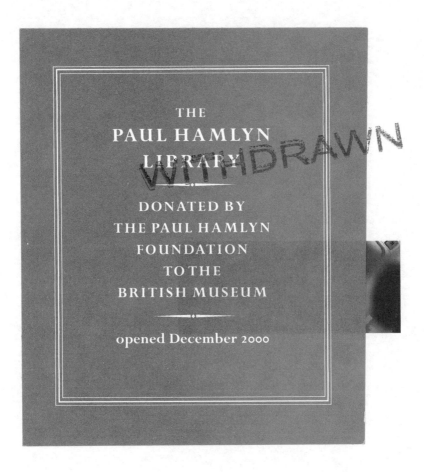

the library and information professional's internet companion

alan poulter

debra hiom

david mcmenemy

facet publishing

© Alan Poulter, Debra Hiom and David McMenemy 2005

Published by
Facet Publishing
7 Ridgmount Street
London WC1E 7AE
www.facetpublishing.co.uk

Facet Publishing is wholly owned by CILIP: the Chartered Institute of Library
and Information Professionals.

First published 2005

British Library Cataloguing in Publication Data
A catalogue record for this book is available from the British Library.

ISBN 1-85604-509-9

Typeset in 10/16pt ATF Clearface and URW Topic by Facet Publishing.
Printed and made in Great Britain by MPG Books Ltd, Bodmin, Cornwall.

contents

introduction: the internet in modern society

INTRODUCTION

The internet, it was predicted, would democratize the world with open and free exchange of information. Al Gore is credited with coining the term 'Information Superhighway' and in his 1992 book, he described a grand vision including ' "the linking of supercomputers, digital libraries", schools, museums, government agencies and the ordinary citizen at home or in the workplace' (Schoechle, 1995, 429). The internet, and increasingly the world wide web, is transforming how people live their lives. From the ability to book everything from theatre tickets to holidays, to the facility of accessing your credit history, and of researching your family tree, there are few aspects of society that are not touched by the medium.

Whether Gore's vision for society has come to pass is an issue that could be widely debated. Feather has argued that, 'the predictions and expectations about how [the information superhighway] would be achieved have proved to be somewhat inaccurate in detail' (Feather, 2004, 74). Indeed, the internet has proved in many ways to be unpredictable. From a position only a few years ago where music publishers treated the medium as an enemy, the explosion of MP3 players has led to a vast new income stream, with the likes of Apple's world wide web-based ITunes service leading the way in modern music supply and consumption.

Despite the arguments that rage about where the internet is taking society, one thing that certainly cannot be challenged is that it has transformed the role of the library and information (LIS) professional. For the profession, it could be argued that the internet revolution has been as profound as that of the printing press. Indeed, as Feather has stated, 'the printed word has already been superseded in some parts of the information market-place' (Feather, 2004, 72). The reach of the internet extends into every aspect of service delivery. The impact on libraries will be discussed later in this book, but consider a few examples:

- selection and renewal of items on loan
- purchasing of stock
- accessing e-journals
- virtual learning environments (VLEs)
- reader development websites.

All of these services have been enhanced by the opportunities the internet provides, and it would be difficult to imagine going back to the days before it streamlined and enhanced such services for the customer. The snapshots discussed below illustrate just how much impact there has been on library services.

SERVICE SNAPSHOTS

The following snapshots are used as illustrations of just how much the internet is at the heart of service provision in the 21st century library. Understanding it is crucial for the modern LIS professional, not merely in providing services that currently exist, but also in developing new services that would have been impossible before this modern revolution. Service development in the information society involves not merely providing access, but creation of content too.

'A question for the enquiry desk'

Martin is stuck with a crossword clue. He cannot find the answer himself using his home computer, which has an internet connection. He lives miles from the nearest town, let alone a public library. What can he do? Now he can ask a reference librarian a question without getting out of his chair.

At Southern University in Illinois the staff of the Morris Library have been experimenting with a service they call Morris Messenger. This is a **virtual** reference service for users using their own developed **instant messaging** (IM) software. Instant messaging (see Chapter 7) allows two or more people to exchange messages: what one person types appears on the screens of other people invited into the messaging. So rather than visit a library, a user can 'talk' directly to a reference librarian, although they could be continents apart.

The decision by the staff at the Morris Library to develop their own IM software was made after evaluation of commercially available packages. The rationale for developing their own was based around the ability to provide an anonymous service for users, as well as being able to rely on their own network for provision of the service. (Desai, 2003, 22). They found that, unlike the formal reference enquiry, where a query is fully explained by the user, 43% of users of the IM reference service type just a keyword or a phrase (Desai, 2003, 25). They were surprised to find that 62% of queries came from users who are actually in the library premises at the time they enter the query! (Desai, 2003, 26).

A survey conducted in 2001 found over 200 library services in the USA that were already using chat reference services, and there is little doubt that this number will have multiplied since then (Francoeur, 2001, 190).

Increasingly, software solutions that provide such services are becoming more common for commercial use as a direct alternative to chat clients like Yahoo! Messenger. Francoeur discusses the various options available on his website, The Teaching Librarian, www.teachinglibrarian.org/. Many libraries have decided to customize software solutions that were originally created for commercial organizations wanting to provide online real time customer services. Francoeur (2002) sees the following benefit in commercial software:

> Not only can the librarian chat live with a user, the librarian can also show things online to the user (by pushing web pages), which is an approximation (albeit limited) of the way a librarian can demonstrate how to use a database or a web search to a user in a face-to-face encounter in the library.

This becomes as close to real interaction as it can be in a 'virtual' world and offers the ability to assist a user through understanding the resource rather than just pointing them to it and letting them get on with it.

'Helping a student find information'

Maria has just received confirmation of research funding for a PhD in social anthropology. She needs to undertake a widespread literature search in her subject area, including:

- published articles
- books and monographs
- working papers and pre-prints
- latest research projects of people working in the field.

Maria is interested in gaining a comprehensive overview of the work that has been undertaken in this area but wants to see the most up-to-date information first to check that the research position she is hoping to take in her PhD hasn't been investigated before. She is most interested in finding articles and working papers before any other types of information. She will need to consult a number of different bibliographic databases, search working paper archives on the web, visit departmental websites to find out what research projects are going on and who the experts are in this field. Maria's department has a limited budget available to researchers for inter-library loan requests: she will need to work out what information is freely available to her through her institution's library and what she will have to consider requesting from outside. Luckily for Maria, her university library provides mediated assistance to users who need to access material from a range of information sources by integrating systems and services to make discovery and access of information a more seamless experience for users.

This has been facilitated by the development of library management systems into customizable **library portals,** for example MetaLib and Encompass (see Chapter 10). These offer a number of applications including combined cross-searching of bibliographic databases with other information such as full-text sources, internet resources, etc., reference linking to get the user from a bibliographic record to the full text of the most appropriate copy, and the ability to aggregate other tools and information. Academic libraries are increasingly moving towards these portal solutions, partly in response to students seemingly preferring to make web search engines rather than the library OPAC their first port of call when looking for information. These systems allow the library to promote (possibly underused) local content combined with remote resources in ways that make sense to the user, and to offer this together with other content of interest (reading lists, course materials, news, etc.).

Anecdotal evidence from case studies, and user testing of early implementations of library portals, suggests that the ability to cross-search a variety of information is much appreciated by users: one institution reported an increase in usage of subscription databases (some by over 1000%!) (Hamblin and Stubbings, 2003). It is unlikely that these library portals will remove the need for assistance and mediation by library staff, but making relevant content searchable from a single interface will go a long way to help users get a handle on the complex information environment that is available to them.

CONCLUSION

This book explains the internet, and the range of services it offers, from the perspective of a library and information professional. The first part of the book covers in depth the scenarios outlined in the above snapshots – instant messaging and portals – and much more, giving a complete picture of internet applications. The second part of the book fills in the background to the snapshots, showing in detail how the internet has affected the different types of library and information unit, and created new types of service.

The chapters that follow provide a discussion of all aspects of the internet of which the information professional should be aware, and aim to impart a broad understanding of this ubiquitous medium, from its history to its current development, and its utilization in libraries across all sectors worldwide.

Whether you need to get to grips with the complexities of the technologies involved, or to learn how to design better quality websites – and use these technologies to deliver information more efficiently to customers – this book should answer your questions.

REFERENCES

Desai, C. M. (2003) Instant Messaging Reference: how does it compare?, *The Electronic Library*, **21** (1), 21–30.

Feather, J. (2004) *The Information Society: a study of continuity and change*, 4th edn, London, Facet Publishing.

Francoeur, S. (2001) An Analytical Survey of Chat Reference Services, *Reference Services Review*, **29** (3), 189–203.

Francoeur, S. (2002) *The Teaching Librarian: web contact centers*, www.teachinglibrarian.org/webcall.htm.

Gore, A. (1992) *Earth in the Balance: ecology and the human spirit*, Boston, MA., Houghton Mifflin.

Hamblin, Y. and Stubbings, R. (2003) *The Implementation of MetaLib and SFX at Loughborough University Library: a case study*, LISU, October, www.jisc.ac.uk/uploaded_documents/Metalibcasestudy.doc.

Schoechle, T. D. (1995) Privacy on the Information Superhighway: will my house still be my castle?, *Telecommunications Policy*, **19** (6), 429–35.

the world wide web

INTRODUCTION

Before we can explore the nature of the **world wide web** (WWW) we need to talk a little bit about networks in general and the internet in particular. One common misconception is that the web and the internet are one and the same thing. They are not.

Files and filenames

A computer network is a set of computers connected so that they can share not only devices (like printers, scanners, etc.) but also files. The internet is a very large network, containing many millions of computers. On many of those computers are computer files that internet users can access. A computer file will have a location on at least one internet site, but may be duplicated at other (**mirror**) sites. Each file has a **filename** (according to the conventions of the computer where it is located) and a **pathname** that defines the **directory** and **subdirectories** in which it is stored, starting from a **root** (initial) directory at its own site. A filename (and the pathname) should (but may not) describe the content of a file. For example, a file entitled 'handbook' in the 'guides' subdirectory of the 'training' directory in the root directory of a particular site would have a pathname:

/training/guides/handbook

which tells us something about the content of the file. All computer files contain information in **digital** form, which is data expressed in binary (zero or one) patterns. The size of files is measured in **bytes**, each of which consists of eight bits (binary digits set either zero or one). Bytes can represent text, images, sound and video. Thus computer files on the internet contain content as varied as the text of the King James Bible, images of the *Beowulf* manuscript, the opening speech from the original Star Trek series, videos of NASA space missions and up-to-the-minute news stories from CNN.

File formats

There are two problems regarding computer files on the internet. One is that they come in many **formats** (ways of storing content). The format of a file is typically denoted by an **extension** which follows the filename itself. Thus, using the example above, the files:

/training/guides/handbook.txt
/training/guides/handbook.doc
/training/guides/handbook.pdf

could all hold the same content but in different formats. Each format requires different software (e.g. a text editor, Microsoft Word etc.) to access it.

For help on identifying and accessing different file formats see the site File Formats, Extensions and Utilities, www.stack.com/file/extension/index.html.

Finding files on a complex network

The other problem relating to computer files on large networks like the internet is not a technical one (like different formats) but an information one. An up-to-date, complete catalogue is needed for the files on each site, and these site catalogues all need to be merged into one union catalogue. This has happened with library materials but not with files on the internet. There are too many of them; they are continually created, changed and removed; and there is no one to do the job of cataloguing, (although subject gateways provide selected cataloguing of parts of the web – see Chapter 9).

When computer networking started, software tools appeared to mitigate this gap by displaying lists of files available, and these allowed information about content to be added. **Bulletin board systems** (BBS) were the first to do this and these pre-date the internet by many years, running on networks connected by phone. Some still exist today and their name lives on as many internet repositories of information are called 'boards'.

For a directory of internet-accessible BBS systems see BBS Corner, www.dmine.com/bbscorner/.

File transfer protocol (FTP), was also used to set up file repositories on the internet (see Chapter 4). Archie was a searchable, centralized database of files available for retrieval by FTP and was the first true internet search engine. For many years BBS and FTP were the only means of accessing files. In the early 1990s the University of Minnesota released a package called Gopher. The gopher is the state animal of Minnesota and it is a small rodent which burrows its way to food. Thus Gopher 'burrowed' to files on the internet. It offered a series of menus which the user navigated to get to a link to the file they wanted. For its time Gopher was revolutionary. It made knowing where a file was stored no longer important, removing an enormous burden from users. However, the menu display was relatively inflexible and unexciting. Gopher was swept away in 1993 by the world wide web, which allowed a flexible and colourful display of links to files to be accessible by a simple click of the mouse. Gopher also had search engines: Veronica and Gopher Jewels being the equivalents of Google and Yahoo! respectively. These have long since disappeared.

WHAT IS THE WORLD WIDE WEB?

The world wide web began as a **hypertext** publishing project at CERN in Geneva, to create a way of accessing research papers via the complex network there. Hypertext is linked text: a highlighted word or phrase in one piece of text, when activated, leads to a different piece of text related to the chosen word or phrase. Hypertext had been a research tool for many years before it found the mainstream via its use in the world wide web.

> For a history of hypertext see the Alt.hypertext FAQ, www.csd.uwo.ca/~jamie/hypertext-faq.html.

WEB BROWSERS

On startup, all browsers display a user-definable **home page** which may be set up by your internet access provider. The links you follow are recorded in a **history list** and there are simple forward and back facilities to retrace your path. All browsers support a **favourites** or **bookmark** facility, whereby you can record interesting pages for future reference. Some browsers allow bookmarks to be configured hierarchically, to allow the structured storage of pages.

You can store pages on the computer which is running your browser by setting the browser to cache pages to disk or using a 'save as' option if your browser has one. Pages which you have cached to disk can be reloaded later without having to be connected to the internet. **Offline**

TIM BERNERS-LEE AND THE EARLY HISTORY OF THE WORLD WIDE WEB

The originator of the world wide web was a British computer scientist. When he arrived at CERN, Tim Berners-Lee was given the job of bringing order to the chaotic arrangement of research papers on the network there. Papers were stored in different formats, on different types of computer. Berners-Lee developed new system he called the 'web' which would:

- deal with all types of file
- work on any type of computer
- be simple to use.

He wrote the first **web browser**, a piece of software that worked in the same way on different computers by using hypertext links to files on a network to retrieve those files. It then made those files on any type of computer. The browser needed to work with another piece of software, a **web server**, which the user did not see but which passed files from the machine it was on to the user's browser for display. For details of Tim Berner-Lee's early work, see his personal home page, www.w3.org/People/Berners-Lee/.

Tim Berners-Lee made his browser (and associated server) software freely available and the 'web' slowly spread in academia, becoming the 'world wide web' (WWW) when institutions around the world were using it. The world wide web really took off in early 1993 when the University of Illinois at Urbana-Champaign made freely available for non-commercial use a browser called Mosaic which ran under popular graphical user interfaces like Microsoft Windows, Macintosh and X-Windows.

Mosaic became the 'acceptable face of the internet' and rapidly began to attract commercial interest. The development team of Mosaic left to start their own company, and produced an even more popular browser, Netscape. Microsoft produced a rival to Netscape, Internet Explorer, which gradually took over as the most popular browser. More recently, Mozilla Firefox, www.mozilla.org/products/firefox/, an **open-source** (its program code is freely available) and distant descendant of Netscape, and Opera, www.opera.com, have appeared to give alternatives to Internet Explorer. For more on the history and current status of web browser software see Browser News, www.upsdell.com/BrowserNews/.

browsers are special browsers which essentially exist not to view sites but to save them to a local disk.

For a list of offline browsers see Offline Browsing Tools, http://directory.google.com/Top/Computers/ Software/Shareware/Windows/Internet/Offline_Browsing_Tools/.

Some browsers allow you to e-mail a page to yourself. If you just want to take a quote or a few lines of text from a web page you can **copy** and **paste** text from the screen by simply highlighting the text and using the edit menu to copy – this can then be pasted into any text document. It is possible to save images alone to disk by right-clicking on the image and following the pop-menu which should appear.

HTML

Hypertext browsing is not without problems, but it offers a number of advantages over inflexible menu structures, as world wide web links can be embedded in text anywhere on a **web page**, i.e. a text file marked up in a language called **hypertext markup language** (HTML). HTML, a derivative of **standard generalized markup language** (SGML), allows the formatting of a page to be controlled by means of **tags**, which indicate the nature of particular page **elements** (title, headings, paragraphs, lists, etc.). See Chapter 2 for more on HTML. It is possible to embed graphics in pages, making them better looking than text-only screens. On the server side, it is easy for people to publish information themselves, because HTML is reasonably straightforward, and software tools for HTML are readily available. Creating personal home pages got many people interested in publishing information on the internet.

URLs

A link to another page or resource is expressed by a **uniform resource** locator (URL), which gives the retrieval method (usually **http**, the hypertext transfer protocol for WWW), the host and domain name and the path and file name of the page to be retrieved. For example, the URL for the Internet Resources Newsletter is:

http://www.hw.ac.uk/libWWW/irn/irn.html

where:

- http is the retrieval method (hypertext transfer protocol)
- www.hw.ac.uk is the host and domain name (Heriot-Watt University, UK)
- libWWW/irn/irn.html is the path and filename (irn.html is a file in the irn directory which is itself in the libWWW directory).

Many URLs end in a slash (/) symbol. This means that the page they refer to has a **default** (expected) name, like home.html or index.html. The names of pages must comply with the file-naming conventions of the computer on which they are kept.

If you have a web browser you can open a link to any page on the internet, providing you know its URL. Use the 'open' command or its equivalent and enter the URL. If you get 'not found' or a similar error message, first check that you have entered the URL *exactly* as it should be, character for character and case for case. There are no spaces in URLs. Don't worry about typing http://, as your browser will automatically add it to the address. If you have not made a mistake, try truncating the URL by omitting characters from the right-hand end, up to the rightmost slash (/). For example, instead of :

www.examplesite.co.uk/magazine/issue23/leadarticle.html

try using:

www.examplesite.co.uk/magazine/issue23/

If your truncated URL still does not work, keep removing the last portion until you reach the slash that precedes the site name. If this still fails there is no point in truncating further. All truncation is doing is looking for higher-level pages at the site in question. If you find a URL that works, you may be able to follow links to the page you want. However, do be prepared for invalid URLs and for URLs which point to non-existent pages. **Linkrot** is the process by which maintainers change the names and locations of pages over time.

> One tip to find old pages now deleted or renamed is to look for them on Archive.org, www.archive.org, an enormous store of copies of web pages taken in the past. Note that not everything is stored there!

It is sometimes possible to guess URLs if you are familiar with the main **domain** types (category of website). For example, the URL for IBM is www.ibm.com/ (not all URLs are so obvious, though). For more on hosts/domains see Chapter 8.

Pages can sometimes take minutes to load. Speed of page retrieval depends partly on where the page is coming from. Retrieving a page from the USA is often slow compared with a European site and may take longer later in the day. Use a local mirror site if you can find one, or choose a time of day that is likely to be quiet at the remote site.

There are two other ways of speeding up page retrieval. The first is to stop your browser loading graphics. Graphics are nice, but take far longer to load than the textual content of pages. The second way to speed things up is to use a **caching proxy**. This is a special computer which stores a copy of the page(s) that you retrieve. If you go back to those pages, or reload them, your browser will load them from the caching proxy computer, and not the original source. You will need to ask your internet access provider about the availability of a caching proxy (most institutions should run one).

HOW TO SEARCH THE INTERNET EFFECTIVELY

As the world wide web developed, it dramatically increased in size and offered more and more functionality. Nobody knows for sure how many web pages there are. Thus following links on world wide web pages can lead you around in circles. The practice of exploring links to see where they lead is known as **surfing** and can be fun. However, for the serious information seeker, better ways of finding useful pages are needed. **Subject listings** and **search engines** are the two main ways to locate information.

Subject listings

Subject listings organize internet resources under subject headings. These listings are sometimes called **directories**, virtual libraries or **subject gateways** but all are generally characterized by the input of human effort into creating these listings. They are typically organized by an alphabetical index or a classification scheme. They contain links to far fewer pages than do search engines, but the links ideally will have been selected for quality. They may contain more than just links to pages; they may have reviews or ratings as well. Another important characteristic is that subject listings generally have a hierarchical structure and cross-referenced subject terms which facilitate information **browsing**. Subject listings services can only be as accurate and comprehensive as the efforts of their compilers allow. This is where listings services with commercial backing or government sponsorship can score over those maintained by volunteers.

In specific areas subject listings can be very useful indeed. However, they will not include everything, sometimes not even the best resources and they may also be out of date.

Probably the most popular of these directory services is the Open Directory Project, http://dmoz.org/, which aims to construct the most comprehensive web directory using the input of several thousand volunteer editors who select and add resources to the service. Yahoo!, http://uk.yahoo.co.uk, used to be predominant here but has neglected to maintain and develop its subject listing services, when compared with the range of other services it offers. Other subject listings are About.com, www.about.com and the Resource Discovery Network, www.rdn.ac.uk/, which is recommended for its collection of academic subject portals (see Chapter 9).

Search engines

A search engine is a website that acts like a huge catalogue of the many pages available on the internet. Each search engine sends out a piece of software, called a **robot**, a **spider** or a **crawler**, to copy pages from the web into its searchable database. Not all pages are copied. Examples of this type are A9, www.a9.com/, Ask Jeeves, www.ask.co.uk/, and WiseNut, www.wisenut.com/.

A user's search words are matched against indexes generated from this database using **relevance ranking** techniques, which aim to retrieve and rank the pages that best match (contain most query words most often) the user's query. High ranked pages appear top of the list of all pages found. How well search engines rank pages is sometimes a matter for speculation: **index spamming** is the practice of trying to raise a page's search ranking by tweaking the content and structure of that page to appeal to ranking algorithms used by particular search engines. Some search engines allow **paid-for listings** in search results, which can distort automatic ranking.

The leading search engine currently is Google, www.google.co.uk. It has eschewed the standard page ranking policy based on word content for a ranking based on links to those pages. Google ranks pages highly on a search topic which have many links labelled for that topic pointing at them, thus attempting to use judgements to link as indications of content quality. While it is not impossible to index spam, this ranking technique generally produces good results.

Search engines collect and maintain enormous databases of web pages and their URLs. Although they devote considerable effort to this task, the rate of growth of new web servers and new web pages makes completeness impossible to achieve. **Freshness** (keeping up with current web page contents) is another impossible goal, again for reasons of volume and volatility. So, while search engines can index billions of web pages (at the time of writing Google has 8 billion pages indexed), it is still estimated that any one search engine covers only 20–30% of the web at best. Because of differing gathering techniques or coverage policies the content of search engines can vary. A page found on one may not be on another, which means that a comprehensive search requires the use of a number of search engines.

A way to avoid repeating a search in many search engines is to use a **meta search engine**, which searches across a number of search engines at the same time and presents the integrated results to you on a single page.

> Recommended meta search engines are Teoma, www.teoma.com, and ZapMeta, www.zapmeta.com. However, meta search engines can do no better than produce results that other search engines would produce.

Invisible web

Search problems do not stop here. First, there is a plethora of search engines that crawl the web for particular topics only, rather than all subjects as the previously mentioned search engines do. Second, search engines only collect and index web pages: there are also databases of materials searchable via a web interface, which never appear in search engine results. These materials are known as the **invisible web** (or **hidden/deep web**). Some search services offer either listings of search engines by their subject speciality or try to access off-web materials again by subject category.

These services can be categorized as **specialist search engines**, in contrast to meta search engines.

Search Engine Guide, www.searchengineguide.com/searchengines.html, and CompletePlanet, www.completeplanet.com/, offer listings by subject speciality, while Invisible-Web.Net, www.invisible-web.net, and Profusion, www.profusion.com/, try to access off-web materials. Google is also working hard to capture some of this hidden web by working directly with academic institutions and publishers. Google Scholar, http://scholar.google.com/, enables users to search specifically for scholarly literature, including peer-reviewed papers, theses, books, preprints, abstracts and technical reports.

Reference sources and discussions

Two other types of search service need mentioning. A lot of information questions boil down to simple topics, e.g. what was the date of the battle of Trafalgar? **Reference sources** (encyclopedias, directories, dictionaries, time-tables, etc.) are ideal for answering straightforward questions. Not all inform-ation is contained on the internet: books, journals, magazines and news-papers are still rich sources of information and can be located via the internet.

Refdesk, www.refdesk.com/, and InfoPlease, www.infoplease.com/, are collections of reference tools while LibrarySpot, www.libraryspot.com, is a gateway to online catalogues.

Information sources so far have all been computer files. People also are accessible via the internet and they can be a valuable source of information. **Discussion sources** work in two ways: either they can lead to answers found in archived discussions or they allow questions to be put to experts who may respond. However, not all discussions are recorded or easily searchable, especially those of mailing lists. Never ask a question without ensuring it is 'on topic' for a discussion forum, reading any frequently asked questions first, and accompanying your question with a detailed history of your search so far, to forestall people thinking you are being lazy!

Search strategies

Six categories of search service (subject listings, search engines, meta

Google Groups, http://groupbeta.google.com/, BoardReader, www.boardreader.com, and Daypop, www.daypop.com/, are archives of, respectively, all Usenet conferences, selected web conferences and web logs (see Chapter 6 for details of these services). Feedster, www.feedster.com, covers RSS feeds (see 'Advanced web technologies' below). Sources of mailing lists (see Chapter 5) on which to ask questions are the National Academic Mailing List Service, www.jiscmail.ac.uk/, and TILE.NET, http://tile.net/lists.

search engines, specialist search engines, reference sources and discussions) have been covered. All the search services that fall into these categories use different procedures for searching – for best results read the help files they provide and get to know their capabilities well. Some very general rules for searching that apply to all of them are:

- Try to be specific with the keywords that you use; if you are interested in photography, specify what area, e.g. composition, equipment, etc. There are millions of web pages out there so generally the more specific you can be the better.
- If your search returns few or no results think about possible synonyms.
- Use the options of combining words with 'and'; searching on 'photography and equipment' will look for documents containing both these terms.
- Some search engines will let you search using 'not'; a search for 'photography not equipment' will look for documents containing the word photography but not containing the word equipment.
- If you are searching for proper names use capitalization; this should narrow down the results. If you type in lower case most search engines will search both upper and lower case words.
- Review your initial search results and refine your search terms if necessary.
- Bookmark relevant results as you go. Check these for links to new sources.

Before you begin you should try to formulate a search strategy to use the multitude of search services in a sensible order, so as to maximize the chance of finding the information required in the minimal amount of time. There is a logical order of use for the six categories given:

Stage 1. Reference sources

It is best to start with a reliable source, i.e. books, journals or reference works. These will answer simple questions or at least give background to the search topic and suggest synonyms/related terms.

Stage 2. Meta search engines

Good for simple queries, so the information wanted may be obtained at this stage, obviating the need for later stages.

Stage 3. Subject listings

A browsing search might succeed where a keyword search has failed.

Stage 4. Search engines

Be sure to make use of any advanced search facilities offered so as to get results missed by meta search engines.

Stage 5. Specialist search engines

These will find either web pages not in general search engines or resources not on the web itself.

Stage 6. Discussion sources

If all else fails try to find a person to ask for an answer, after checking that no answer exists in online discussions.

Finally, remember that searching the internet is an activity that continually changes, as new search services appear (and disappear) over time.

Search Engine Watch, www.searchenginewatch.com, provides news of the developing capabilities of existing search services as well as reviews of new services.

ADVANCED WEB TECHNOLOGIES
Plug-ins and streaming

The world wide web not only expanded extremely rapidly in size, but changed to incorporate new or co-opted technologies, giving it more and more functionality. URLs can be used to retrieve and deliver sound and video by means of **plug-ins** (extra software modules in a browser which act on a specific file type).

Download.com, www.download.com/Plug-ins/3150-2378-0.html?tag=dir, maintains a listing of plug-ins, sortable by number of downloads to reveal the most popular.

Some plug-ins are for playing sound and video files, which have to be downloaded in their entirety before they can be played. An alternative is **streaming**, the sending of a continuous flow of data, typically sound or video, formatted in such a way as to preserve as much quality as possible across the internet.

Microsoft, Real Networks and Apple offer different streamed formats. For free plug-ins for these formats, see respectively: www.microsoft.com/windows/windowsmedia/9Series/GettingStarted/home.asp, http://uk.real.com/radiopass/ and www.apple.com/quicktime/.

Streaming can be used to allow radio and television stations to broadcast globally via the internet. For a directory of available channels, see Liveradiotv, www.pcjb.com/Liveradiotv.html.

Another way to generate media content is to use a **web cam**, a static camera trained on a view of a place, etc. The first web cam showed a coffee machine in a research lab in Cambridge University. The Trojan Room Coffee Machine, www.cl.cam.ac.uk/coffee/coffee.html, enabled researchers to know when coffee was available! For a global listing of web cams, see 123cam All Cam Live, www.123cam.com/.

Media content

As well as textual information on web pages, the web has become the premier repository of media-based information – images, sound and video.

Recommended for media searches are:
- for images: Google Image Search, http://images.google.com/ Altavista Image Search, www.altavista.com/image/default Yahoo! Image Search, http://search.yahoo.com.images
- for audio files: Audiophilez, www.audiophilez.com/
- for audio/video files: Singingfish, www.singingfish.com/
- for video files: Yahoo! Video Search, http://video.search.yahoo.com/ Blinkx Video Search, www.blinkx.tv/.

One way of finding media files is to do a standard search and then look for images, etc. in the pages found. Increasingly, however, search engines allow searches for media clips alongside general searches.

RSS, wikis and dynamic pages

Web is a **pull** technology: it is up to the user to seek out and 'pull' a web page into their browser. **Push** content comes to the user. An **RSS feed** is a way of implementing push technology for the world wide web. RSS (**rich site summary**, also known as **really simple syndication**), www.rss-specifications.com, is a method for notification of new or changed page content. It is an application of **XML** (for more information, see Chapter 2). A special **RSS reader** software package can accumulate notifications and announce them to a user, saving the user having to hunt for new content.

Download.com maintains a list of RSS readers at www.download.com/RSS-Tools/ 3150-9227_4-0.html?tag=dir. RSS Express, http://rssxpress.ukoln.ac.uk/, works via a standard web browser and gives a listing of UK-sourced RSS feeds. A good global directory of RSS feeds is Syndic8, www.syndic8.com/.

A **wiki** is a collection of web pages over which a group has collective editing rights. It is ideal for collaborative working on the web.

> The most famous wiki application is the Wikipedia, www.wikipedia.org/, which is a volunteer effort to create an all-encompassing multi-lingual encyclopedia for the internet.

Standard world wide web pages consisting of HTML coding are **static**: they have only one appearance/function. Including program code in pages can make them **dynamic**, i.e. change in response to input from a user, and can greatly extend their functionality. Javascript is a programming language developed especially for use in WWW pages. Its big brother is Java, a revolutionary programming language which can provide the same functionality on any computer system that can run a browser. These are known as client-side programming languages, in that they run in a user's browser and not on a remote server. For more on dynamic web pages, see Chapter 2.

Using these languages, it is possible to deliver just about any computer application via the world wide web, leading to the concept of the **network computer**, a computer which in itself is devoid of storage and function, but can be activated by software, etc. from the world wide web. While network computers have not caught on, a wide range of applications, from calendars to complete accounting systems, can be delivered over the internet via a web browser. Companies providing a complete suite of applications software are known as **application service providers** (ASPs).

> For a listing of ASPs see The List – the Definitive ASP Buyer's Guide, http://asp.thelist.com/.

Simpler applications, many of which are free, are bookmark managers, calendars and file and photo storage.

> Yahoo! is particularly good at providing these functions. See Everything Yahoo!, http://uk.yahoo.com/more.html.

DOWNLOADING SOFTWARE FROM THE WEB

As well as online applications, there is an enormous amount of desktop software available for download through the web. Commercial software, **shareware** (software available for trial before purchase) and **freeware** (free software) are available via the internet. Many non-commercial packages are as good as their commercial (and more expensive) counterparts. There are two ways of obtaining this software.

One way is to browse and search specific websites which hold software. To reduce traffic on the internet, mirrors (local copies of important file archives) exist in most countries: in the UK it is SUNsite Northern Europe, www.sunsite.org.uk/.

Other important software collections are Download.com, www.download.com, The Ultimate Collection of Winsock Software, Tucows, www.tucows.com, and Shareware.com, www.shareware.com.

The other way of obtaining software is to simply search for it using standard search engines. If you know the name of the package (or function) you want, try an internet search for that name (or function). If you know the company which produces the software, try to go to its site, usually at www.[companyname].com.

File compression

Much downloadable software comes in the form of **compressed** files (stored with all redundant data removed) which must be **uncompressed** (or 'unpacked') before installation. To compress and de-compress files special software is needed. Media files, as well, come in compressed format so installing a range of de/compression software is useful!

Usually one of the uncompressed files in a software download is called 'setup' or 'install' and running (double clicking) on this file normally starts the installation process.

> The commonest file compression software used is WinZip, www.winzip.com, but there are others, see http://directory.google.com/Top/Computers/Software/Data_Compression/.

BUYING FROM THE WEB

Yahoo! has already been mentioned above in relation to searching the internet and supplying applications. However, an examination of Yahoo! will reveal that this is not all that it offers. It has meeting places, like conferencing areas, e-mail accounts, chat lines and online games. It also functions like a newspaper, offering world and local news along with sports, film reviews, etc. All these elements are built into one simple screen. This particular mixture of services, as exemplified by Yahoo!, is known as a **portal**, because it serves as a simple gateway into the complexity of the world wide web.

> Yahoo! is currently the most successful single portal but it is being chased by AOL (America Online), www.aol.co.uk, and MSN (MicroSoft Network), www.msn.co.uk.

The top portals are overwhelmingly the first internet destination of most internet users. Portals try to be **sticky**, that is hold onto surfers and, if possible, make them spend money. Portals have a strong element of **e-business**, both in advertising on screen but also in links to online shops, auction rooms and classified advertising.

E-business sites fall into one of two categories, **pureplay**, existing only on the web, or **clicks and mortar**, having both a web and a high street presence. Ebay, www.ebay.co.uk, is an example of a pureplay site. It is an auction site and uses the mass of people on the web to fuel auction activities with enormous numbers of buyers and sellers. Ebay creates a service that never existed before. Another example of a new business is Lastminute.com, www.lastminute.com/, which sells a range of products and services in the very last available time slot. Amazon, www.amazon.co.uk, duplicates the function of bookshops, music stores, toyshops, etc. but brings together a much vaster range of products than any physical shop could. In the **dot com boom** of the late 1990s, a rash of pureplay sites collapsed as they failed to establish themselves as either brands or needed services. Clicks and mortar sites are set up by established businesses and do pretty much what that business does away from the web. For example, Tesco.com, www.tesco.com, adds a home delivery function to Tesco's supermarket business.

As a result, the online shopper is faced with a large number of shopping sites, some with established names, others with names which are deliberately intended to be different and function-free. Just as with search services, there are meta shopping services which search a range of online shops for prices on comparable products and services, for example Kelkoo, www.kelkoo.co.uk. However, there is a bewildering number of meta shopping services (see http://directory.google.com/Top/Regional/ Europe/United_Kingdom/Recreation_and_Sports/ Home_and_Garden/Consumer_Information/Price_Comparisons/) and online shops, so the online consumer is faced with a massive choice problem, which shopping in the high street or mall cannot emulate.

Another problem for the online consumer is trust. Trust is needed to buy and sell from individuals you will never meet on Ebay or to buy from a website which you have never seen before and which has no 'street' presence. Trust is also needed to enter credit card details into online

> There is plenty of advice for the online shopper, for example Consumer Direct, www.consumerdirect.gov.uk/.

shopping carts (forms for recording purchase details). The transactional risks of online shopping, however, are minimal and many problems stem from the novelty of the medium and the poor design of many shopping sites.

See Chapter 8 for more information on how secure shopping works.

creating web pages

INTRODUCTION

The previous chapter introduced you to HTML and the web; this chapter looks at the fundamentals of creating web pages and points you to useful tutorials and tools that can help you explore this area further.

In any browser it is possible to view the HTML source of a web page. It is necessary to understand how HTML works to be able to build web pages. One great way of learning HTML is to see a good web page and view its source to see how it was constructed. But to do this you need a grounding in HTML.

BASIC WEB PAGES

Hypertext markup language (HTML) is a platform-independent language that enables web browsers to display files in a standard format on a monitor. The basic component of the language is a **tag**, which informs the browser how to display data, for instance describing the size, style and positioning in the document. In publishing terms these specifications are called **markup**.

Apart from a few exceptions, tags come in pairs, an opening and closing tag, which encapsulate the text to be displayed in a

> The most current specification of HTML is Version 4,
> www.w3.org/TR/REC-html40/.

particular style. The opening and closing tag are almost identical apart from the forward slash (/) in the closing tag. For example, the following HTML statement:

```
<B>The Internet</B> is the fastest growing
computer network in the world.
```

will be displayed in a browser as:

> **The Internet** is the fastest growing
> computer network in the world.

as the paired <B></B> tags produce a bold-face type.

Page elements

Every HTML document must contain some standard tags to define its major components:

- <HTML> and </HTML> indicate the beginning and end of an HTML document. An HTML document consists of a heading section and a body section.
- The heading section mostly contains the **title** of the document that will be displayed in the title section by the browser. The heading section is identified by the tags <HEAD> and </HEAD>, and the title tags are <TITLE> and </TITLE>.
- The body section contains the main text and images of the document, and is identified by <BODY> and </BODY>.

A basic HTML document will therefore look something like this:

```
<HTML>
<HEAD>
<TITLE>My home page</TITLE>
</HEAD>
<BODY>
This web page will contain information about me.
</BODY>
</HTML>
```

Adding text to the body of a web page simply causes that text to be displayed as a solid body. There are many tags that allow you to format the text in your document. A few of these formatting tags are described below.

Headings and formatting

Physical style tags

Headings are used to indicate new sections and subsections with tags like <H1> and </H1>. HTML offers six heading levels numbered <H1> to <H6>, where <H1> is used for the main heading, and <H6> for the lowest level of heading.

Paragraphs can be defined using just <P>, and indicate a block of text. This is relevant as a browser ignores any hard returns (carriage returns or line breaks), indentations or blank lines in HTML documents. This feature also enables you to lay out your source text in such a way that is easy to read for you, e.g. starting each tag on a new line.

The centre tags <CENTER> and </CENTER> can be used to centre items, for example:

```
<CENTER>This is a centred paragraph.<P></CENTER>
```

will be displayed in a browser as:

> This is a centred paragraph.

Text can be formatted as bold by using the <B> and </B> tags, as italics by using the <I> and </I> tags, and underlined by using the <U> and </U> tags. Note that underlines are used by default to indicate links.

Logical style tags

Logical style tags format text according to the meaning of its attributes on the browser style sheet. For instance the logical style element <EM> for emphasis would generally be displayed as italics, unless defined differently on the style sheet. Common logical style tags are:

- <EM> and </EM> for emphasis (usually displayed as italics)
- <STRONG> and </STRONG> for strong emphasis (usually displayed as bold)
- <CITE> and </CITE> for citation (usually displayed as italics).

If you want to include a line break with no extra space between lines (such as the <P> tag would define) you can use the <BR> tag. This is one of the few tags that does not require a closing tag. For example:

```
Line one<BR>Line two
```

will be displayed in a browser as:

Line one
Line two

A horizontal black line can be added after a section of text with the single <HR> tag (horizontal rule).

Colour

You can change the background colour by adding an attribute to the <BODY> tag. For example, <BODY BGCOLOR="BLUE"> will change the background to blue. The colour of text can be changed by modifying the <BODY> tag to read, for instance, <BODY TEXT="RED">. These tags can be combined into one tag, for instance <BODY BGCOLOR="RED" TEXT="BLACK">.

Note the US spelling of the BGCOLOR tag!

Colours are represented either by their names or as a six-digit hexadecimal value, showing **RGB** (red/green/blue) values (see below).

You can find sample colours and their values at Mediarama's Color Page Builder, www.inquisitor.com/hex.html.

Lists
Unnumbered lists

To create unnumbered lists, which use bullet points, use the paired tags <UL> and </UL> which encapsulate a number of list items, identified by the single tag <LI>. For example:

```
<UL>
<LI> first item
<LI> second item
<LI> third item
</UL>
```

will be displayed in a browser as:

- first item
- second item
- third item

Numbered lists

Numbered lists (or ordered lists) are created in exactly the same way as unnumbered lists but require the tag pairs <OL> and </OL>, which encapsulate a number of list items <LI>.

Nested lists

Lists can be nested (contain other lists) by using embedded list tags. For example:

```
<UL>
<LI> first item
<UL>
<LI> first subitem
<LI> second subitem
</UL>
<LI> second item
```

```
<LI> third item
</UL>
```

will be displayed in a browser as:

- first item
  - o first subitem
  - o second subitem
- second item
- third item

Links and anchors

The hypertext element of HTML enables you to create **links** to different parts of the same document, or to other documents. These hyperlinks can be text or an image and can usually be identified because they are a different colour, are underlined or the cursor changes to the pointed finger.

A hyperlink to another document needs to contain instructions on how to find the linked-to document. This can be an **absolute pathname** (document locator on another machine), for example a full URL such as www.someuniversity.ac.uk/webdirectory/filename.html, or a **relative pathname** (document locator on the same machine as the web page), such as diskdirectory/filename.html. Relative pathnames contain no machine identifier, therefore the local filestore is assumed as the target of the link.

The complete hyperlink format is:

```
<A HREF="pathname">This text will be underlined as
a link</A>
```

where <A> is the opening anchor tag for a hyperlink, and within that tag HREF is followed by the pathname to the linked-to file. In this example, in a browser the text "This text will be underlined as a link" will be highlighted, and </A> is the end anchor tag. The hyperlink format for absolute pathnames is:

```
<A HREF="http://www.someuniversity.ac.uk/
webdirectory/filename.html">This link goes to
filename.html at SomeUniversity</A>
```

For relative pathnames it will be:

```
<A HREF="diskdirectory/filename.html">This link
goes to filename.html on this computer</A>
```

Hyperlinks can also be used to link to a specific section of a document. To do this, the specific sections need to have **named anchors** to which the links can refer. These named anchors are created by including the tags <A NAME> and </A>. For instance, to create a link within a document, first place the named anchor:

```
<A NAME="sechead1">Section Heading One</A>
```

where Section Heading One has now been named the identifier. This will enable the creation of a link to the section as follows:

```
<A HREF="#sechead1">This link goes to Section
Heading One</A>
```

where in a browser the hyperlink "This link goes to Section Heading One" will link to Section Heading One.

The two techniques of linking can be combined, as in the following hyperlink:

```
<A HREF="http://www.someuniversity.ac.uk/
webdirectory/filename.html#sechead1"> Underlined
link to Section Heading One in filename.html at
SomeUniversity</A>
```

Good tutorials on basic HTML include:
- The Basics, www.htmlgoodies.com/primers/basics.html
- Getting Started with HTML, www.w3.org/MarkUp/Guide/
- HTML Tutorial, www.w3schools.com/html/default.asp.

WEB PAGE GRAPHICS

A computer display projects various intensities of red, green and blue light onto each **pixel** (picture element) on a screen. Hence colours can be defined by values for red/green/blue (**RGB**) combinations. Images are formed out of pixels. **Bitmap** (aka raster) image-file formats record images in terms of the pixels to display. They can be edited by altering the pixels directly with a **bitmap editor**.

Bitmap images

However, bitmap image formats tend to have large file sizes, making them unsuitable for sending over the internet. The two most common web image formats are the **graphics interchange format** (GIF) and the **joint photographic experts group** (JPEG). Both compromise the image for the sake of **compression** (saving storage space by not storing redundant image data), so these formats should not be used to store original, high-quality artwork that is to be modified later. JPEG works very well for photographic images with gradual colour changes and no sharp edges. GIF works best for simple line images. GIF has a few unique features: it has limited transparency, so that one colour in an image's palette can be designated as **transparent**. An **interlaced** GIF, instead of being transmitted and displayed top-to-bottom like a normal image, is first displayed at its full size with a very low resolution, then at a higher resolution, until it finally attains a normal appearance. Also a GIF file can contain several images, along with a duration value for each one, to produce **animation**.

For information on creating animated GIFs, see the site GIF Animation Tools, www.wdvl.com/Multimedia/Animation/GIF/.

Vector images

The alternative to the bitmap image format is the vector image, which records images in terms of geometric shapes. These shapes are converted to bitmaps for display on the monitor. Vector images are easier to modify, because the components can be moved, resized, rotated or deleted independently. Macromedia's Flash, www.macromedia.com/software/flash/, is the closest thing to a standard vector format on the web. The **World Wide Web Consortium (W3C)** has designed a true image format that can also be used on the web, the portable network graphic (PNG), www.w3.org/TR/REC-png.html.

The Technical Advisory Service for Images (TASI), www.tasi.ac.uk/index.html, and Graphics on the Web, www.w3.org/Graphics/. are good sites for information about images.

The HTML tag used to include an image in a web page is:

```
<IMG SRC="image.gif">
```

The above example assumes that your graphics file image.gif is in exactly the same directory as your web page. If it is not then you need to precede the graphics filename with a directory path. An image can become the source of a link using the following HTML:

```
<A HREF="http://www.someuniversity.ac.uk/webdirectory/
filename.html"><IMG SRC="image.gif"></A>
```

You can specify how text and image should be aligned. By default following text will align with the bottom of the image. You can also specify top and middle alignment using the following formats:

```
<IMG SRC="image.gif" ALIGN=TOP> Text to be displayed
```

```
<IMG SRC="image.gif" ALIGN=MIDDLE>Text to be
displayed
```

You can change the background to a graphic (GIF or JPG) file. The <BODY> tag will become <BODY BACKGROUND="image.gif">. Note that this overrides a BGCOLOR setting.

PAGE LAYOUT AND STRUCTURE

HTML provides instructions to the web browser about the content of a page as well as how information should be displayed on screen, for example the size or colour of the text . When starting to design the layout and structure of a page it is worth bearing in mind that there are some things that you, as an author, can't control, such as:

- the user's browser which may display HTML in slightly different ways
- the size of the browser window
- the user's speed of connection to the internet.

Taking these into consideration you should aim to keep your web pages short and simple. The following sections detail some ways of structuring and laying out content within a web page.

Tables

Tables can be a powerful way of laying out content on web pages. Think of the tabular structures that underlie printed pages in newspapers, books, magazines, etc. Tables enable vertical and horizontal structure to a page especially when table borders are made invisible. Pick a website and chances are you will see a table being used for formatting.

Tables are defined in HTML by the <TABLE> and </TABLE> tags. A table can be given a border as an attribute of the <TABLE> tag, for instance <TABLE BORDER="1">, where 1 indicates the line thickness; 0 indicates an invisible border and is useful for concealing the use of a table in formatting content on a web page. Rows are defined by <TR> and </TR> tags at the beginning and end of each row. Within table rows you can define individual cells with the <TD> and </TD> tags.

A simple table may be defined as follows:

```
<TABLE BORDER="1">
<TR>
        <TD>item 1</TD>
```

```
            <TD>item 2</TD>
    </TR>
    <TR>
            <TD>item 3</TD>
            <TD>item 4</TD>
    </TR>
    </TABLE>
```

It will be displayed in a browser as:

Item 1	Item 2
Item 3	Item 4

In the following example table, the <WIDTH> value of 100% makes a table fill the available browser screen: resizing the browser will automatically resize the table and preserve formatting. Cells will automatically be spaced proportionally to their number (e.g. two cells will each take up 50% of a row). However, this can be overridden by width values for cells (e.g. 75%/25% for two cells in a row). <ALIGN> values for content for each cell can be left, right, center (note American spelling), top or bottom. <COLSPAN> and <ROWSPAN> can be used to merge cells in columns/rows respectively:

```
<TABLE BORDER="1" WIDTH="100%">
<TR>
<TD ALIGN="CENTER">HEADLINE
</TD>
</TR>
<TR>
<TD WIDTH="75%" ALIGN="LEFT" ROWSPAN="2">Lead Story
</TD>
<TD ALIGN="LEFT">Second story
</TR>
<TR>
<TD ALIGN="LEFT">Third story
</TR>
</TABLE>
```

will be displayed in a browser as:

```
┌──────────────────────────────────────────────────────────┐
│                        HEADLINE                            │
├──────────────────────────────┬─────────────────────────────┤
│ Lead story                   │ Second story                │
│                              │                             │
│                              │                             │
│                              ├─────────────────────────────┤
│                              │ Third story                 │
│                              │                             │
│                              │                             │
│                              │                             │
└──────────────────────────────┴─────────────────────────────┘
```

A good introduction to designing tables can be found on the World Wide Web Consortium (W3C) site Tables in HTML Documents, www.w3.org/TR/html401/struct/tables.html.

Frames

Another method of partitioning a web page is **frames**. Frames are individual, independently scrolling regions of a web page. Useful applications of frames are where a static frame displays a page that is always visible while the content in the other frame(s) change; or a frame with a table of contents which links to pages, which will be displayed in an adjacent frame. Up until recently some browsers couldn't display framed pages properly; while this is no longer the case, there are still a number of problems associated with the use of frames, such as printing (users often have to choose to print the frame navigation separately to the page content) and displaying frames within basic web browsers, such as those on PDAs.

A minimum of three HTML files are needed to create a web page containing two frames, one file for each of the frames and another file which defines how the frames fit into the web page: this file is called the **frameset** file. This HTML document is often very simple; it defines the layout of the frames that make up the page using the <FRAMESET> and </FRAMESET> tags. In this document you define how you want the frames to be divided on the screen, and you specify which HTML document you want displayed in each of the frames. To divide the screen in two columns use the <COLS> tag followed by the percentages of the screen you want each column to occupy, for instance:

```
<FRAMESET COLS="30%,70%">
```

will create two columns, the left one occupying 30% of the screen, and the right one the remainder. Similarly, screens can be split horizontally using the <ROWS> tag. Frames can be further split using nested frames. The <FRAMESET> tag can be further modified with the border and frameborder attributes to include visible lines around frames, for example:

```
<FRAMESET BORDER=1 FRAMEBORDER=1 COLS="30%,70%>
```

To display HTML documents in a frame the single <FRAME> tag is used for each of the frames. The format is:

```
<FRAME SRC="fileone.html" NAME="contentpage"
SCROLLING="NO">
```

```
<FRAME SRC="filetwo.html" NAME="mainwindow"
SCROLLBARS="AUTO">
```

The first column will display the HTML document fileone.html that contains a page of contents, and has been named contentpage. No scrollbar will be displayed in this window. The second column will display HTML document filetwo.html that contains the main text, and which has been named mainwindow. Scrollbars will be used if necessary. A frameset is an HTML page that simply lists how many frames are shown and initially what pages are shown within each frame.

A typical HTML document for a frameset, called frameset.html, will be:

```
<HTML>
<HEAD>
</HEAD>
<BODY>
<FRAMESET COLS="20%,80%">
<FRAME SRC="left.html" NAME="left_window"
SCROLLING="no">
<FRAME SRC="index.html" NAME="right_window">
</FRAMESET>
</BODY>
</HTML>
```

Note how each window in the frame is named, so that links can be made to change the page displayed in these windows if wanted.

Assuming files left.html and index.html exist, the containing file frameset.html will be displayed in a browser as:

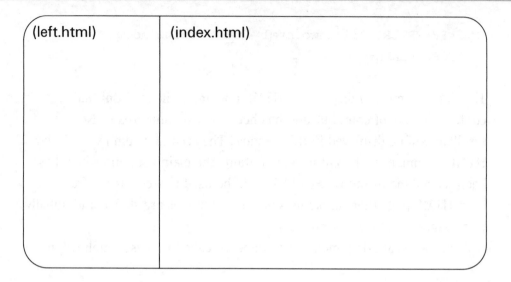

Assume the contents of file left.html are:

```
<HTML>
<HEAD>
</HEAD>
<BODY>
<A HREF="chap1.html" TARGET="right_window">Click here
to see Chapter One</A><P>
<A HREF="chap2.html" TARGET="right_window">Click here
to see Chapter Two</A><P>
</BODY>
</HTML>
```

The above left.html file will appear in the left window of the frameset. It contains two links that will change the contents of the right window, using the **target** attribute, to display different chapters:

(left.html)	(chap1.html or chap2.html, depending on which link is clicked)
Click here to see Chapter One Click here to see Chapter Two	

For a basic tutorial on creating framed pages, see Basic Frames, www.yourhtmlsource.com/frames/basicframes.html.

Style sheets

So far our web pages have been using one font, one text colour, etc. **Cascading style sheets** (CSS) are a feature in HTML that allows fonts, colours, margins, alignments, etc. to be set for both existing HTML tags and user-defined extensions to tags. The advantage of style sheets is that they are normally saved separately from your HTML documents but can control the look and feel of all your pages: by changing your CSS file you can make changes to the appearance of all your documents.

Note that some (older) browsers cannot handle style sheets. Any instructions in a style sheet that a browser cannot handle (e.g. unusual font type) will be ignored and the standard default used instead.

TIP

The following example shows how to use a style sheet:

```
<HTML>
<HEAD>
<TITLE>CSS example</TITLE>
<STYLE TYPE="text/css">
H1 {font-family: Arial; font-style: italic; font-size:
48; color: #00ff00; text-align: center;}
P {color: yellow; font-size: 20}
</STYLE>
</HEAD>
<BODY>
<H1>A green Arial font 48pt italic centred header</H1>
<P>Yellow 20pt text, Mary had a little lamb</P>
</BODY>
</HTML>
```

Note the style sheet declaration – text/css denotes a style sheet which follows the CSS standard. This declaration is enclosed in STYLE tags and comes in the HEAD part of an HTML document. After the tags H1 and P comes a style sheet i.e. a list of style declarations. These ought to be self-explanatory.

Note the American spelling of some style attributes and the hexadecimal number for text colour.

Styles can also be defined for user-defined classes of existing tags. For example, the P (paragraph) tag can have sub-classes first, last, important, bold, italic, etc. and each of these can have a style sheet to give it the required properties. Note that the style sheet for the parent tag (in this case P) is used and is modified by the extra/different properties in the class style sheet (i.e. a 20 point font-size). See the following example:

```
<HTML>
<HEAD>
<TITLE>CSS example 1</TITLE>
<STYLE TYPE="text/css">
H1 {font-family: Arial; font-style: italic; font-
size: 48; color: #00ff00; text-align: center;}
P {color: yellow; font-size: 20}
P.first {color:blue; }
</STYLE>
</HEAD>
<BODY>
<H1>A green Arial font 48pt italic centred header</H1>
<P CLASS="first">This is a blue text first paragraph.
Otherwise it is the same as following
paragraph.</P>
<P>Yellow 20pt text, Mary had a little lamb, testing
testing, 1, 2, 3
etc.</P>
</BODY>
</HTML>
```

A problem with **internal** style sheets, i.e. style sheet declarations contained within a page, is that if we wish to change a style property then we have to edit every page containing that style property. The solution is to use an **external** style, i.e. have our style properties in a file external to the page itself, and reference this external style sheet from the page. Thus, changing one style property in an external style sheet will change that property in every page that references that style sheet. Note that styles defined internally to a page will override definitions in external style sheets, hence the name 'cascading' style sheets, in which documents inherit a basic style but can impose changes if they wish.

Below is an example external style sheet file called mystyles.css. It contains the styles previously used internally:

```
<STYLE TYPE="text/css">
H1 {font-family: Arial; font-style: italic; font-
size: 48; color: #00ff00; text-align: center;}
P {color: yellow; font-size: 20;}
P.first {color:blue;}
</STYLE>
```

Here is our main HTML page, now containing a reference to the external style sheet mystyles.css:

```
<HTML>
<HEAD>
<TITLE>CSS example 2</TITLE>
<LINK REL="stylesheet" TYPE="text/css"
HREF="mystyles.css">
</HEAD>
<BODY>
<H1>A green Arial font 48pt italic centred header</H1>
<P CLASS="first">This is a blue text first paragraph.
Otherwise it is the same as following paragraph.</P>
```

```
<P>Yellow 20pt text, Mary had a little lamb</P>
</BODY>
</HTML>
```

> To learn more about using cascading style sheets see the CSS Tutorial site, www.w3schools.com/css/default.asp.

PAGE CREATION TOOLS

There are hundreds of tools available to help you create web pages. They range from simple text editors to sophisticated software packages that manage the whole process from web page creation to publishing and managing websites.

If you want to create only a handful of pages it is probably not worth splashing out on specialized software when you can use a simple **text editor**. This will involve getting to grips with the fundamental basics of HTML (see previous section) but it will mean that you have control over the HTML that you create.

> Some of the most popular text editing tools include Programmer's File Editor (PFE), www.lancs.ac.uk/staff/steveb/cpaap/pfe/default.htm, TextPad, www.textpad.com/products/textpad/index.html, and UltraEdit, www.ultraedit.com/.

WYSIWYG (what you see is what you get) page creation tools are similar to using a word processor: they hide the technical details of the HTML from the user, who simply chooses from menus how they would like the text to look. However, the HTML code produced by some of these tools is not always standards compliant, which could mean that your web page is not displayed properly in all browsers.

> Some popular WYSIWYG page creation tools include DreamWeaver, www.macromedia.com/software/dreamweaver/, FrontPage, www.microsoft.com/frontpage/, and Fusion, www.netobjects.com/products/html/nf5.html. Web Page Creation Software, www.download.com/Web-Page-Creation/2001-10247_4-0.html?tag=dir, contains a definitive listing of hundreds of web page creation tools.

Whichever tool you choose to create your web pages it is still well worth understanding the basics of HTML so that you can check (and correct) the HTML code you produce.

DYNAMIC WEB PAGES

Dynamic web pages are created only when requested by a browser. In a **static** web page, the HTML and the content of the page have to be created in advance and then stored on a web server. You have been learning to create static web pages. When a user requests that web page, a copy is sent as is. The user can only view the page and cannot alter it in any way. Thus it is said to be 'static', as its content is fixed and determined before viewing and cannot be changed by the user during or after viewing. There are two basic approaches for creating dynamic web pages: one is to create the web page within the browser (**client-side**), and the other is to create the web page on the web server (**server-side**).

In the latter case a program or an application on a web server creates a page by wrapping content in appropriate HTML tags. Creating such program code on the web server is called **server-side scripting**. The program code does its job and passes the results back to the web server in the form of a web page, which the web server returns to the browser on the client's machine. Server-side scripting technologies are vital in integrating web servers and web technology with other software applications and information resources. Many mainstream web services use server-side scripting to pull content from databases (for example, databases of products) and present it to users: Amazon.com works this way. There are disadvantages to server-side scripting: they are adversely affected by slow network speeds between the user and the server and by overloading of the server itself. We will return to server-side scripting later, but will first investigate client-side programming.

CLIENT-SIDE PROGRAMMING

Client-side programming describes programs or scripts that are designed to run within the browser on the user's machine. Some typical uses for this approach are rollover information on images or text, filling out and error checking forms and opening new browser windows. The client-side program has to be downloaded, along with its containing web page. This can be a disadvantage in terms of extra data to transfer, but the pay-off is in greater flexibility in your web pages and the fact that all of the computing load is not served from a single server. It is worth noting that some organizations don't allow client-side scripting on their networks because it is a possible security risk.

Javascript and DHTML

JavaScript is an example of a client-side scripting language. It was originally developed for use in the Netscape browser. Although it is now platform independent not all browsers support this technology, especially adaptive or text-only browsers. JavaScript is generally embedded directly into the <HEAD> of your web page using a <Script> tag.

> If you are interested in learning more about how JavaScript works, take a look at the JavaScript Tutorial, www.w3schools.com/js/default.asp.

If you would like to introduce some interactivity into your web pages without programming you can use a WYSWIG editor such as Dreamweaver to insert some preset JavaScript functions into the page. Alternatively, you could download (and amend if necessary) existing JavaScript programs from online libraries and use them in your own web pages.

> The best site for downloading existing JavaScript programs is the JavaScript Source, http://javascript.internet.com/.

There is a difference between dynamic web pages and a technology called **Dynamic HTML**. Dynamic HTML (DHTML) is not a W3C defined standard in the way that the specification for HTML is; instead it is a way of combining Javascript, cascading style sheets and HTML to provide more client-side interactivity within web pages.

Taylor's Dynamic HTML Tutorial,
http://webmonkey.wired.com/webmonkey/authoring/dynamic_html/tutorials/tutorial1.html, gives a useful introduction to DHTML.

Java

Despite the similarity in name **Java** is not the same as JavaScript. Java is a much more complicated programming language from Sun Microsystems that is designed to be downloadable and run safely on the user's computer without the worry of viruses. Small Java programs are called **applets**: they are commonly used to allow web pages to contain animations, calculators and other functions. A programmer will write a program in Java using some type of Java development software. Once the program is written, they will compile it to produce an applet. Note that applets do not contain readable Java code, rather executable code. Applet files have a .class

The best place to get Java applets is the JavaBoutique,
http://javaboutique.internet.com/.

extension to identify them. The Java language itself is quite complex, so non-programmers will find it difficult to create applets. However, because it is complex, it is far more powerful than JavaScript. You can download many free Java applets on the web. There are clocks, calculators, spreadsheets, search tools and many others.

Note that most Java applets are stored compressed. You will need to uncompress them before using them (see Chapter 1 for more on compression). Some of the Java applets on the web come with **source code**, i.e. the readable version of Java applets. Programming Java involves writing programs in Java source code and then compiling these programs into Java applet form. There are free programming tools (Java development kits) available for Java programming.

For some excellent beginner-level tutorials on programming in Java, see the Tutorials site, http://dmoz.org/Computers/Programming/Languages/Java/FAQs,_Help,_and_Tutorials/Tutorials/Beginner_Level/.

SERVER-SIDE SCRIPTING

Server-side scripting describes any programs or scripts that are carried out by the web server. Just as with client-side programming, there is a variety of available technologies. All web servers come with a special **common gateway interface** (CGI) capability. A version of Java, **Java servlets**, can also be used for server-side scripting. **Active server pages** (ASP) and **server side includes** (SSI) are also used for server-side scripting.

SSI

SSIs (server side includes) are a way to include information into your HTML pages at the time they are requested by a client or browser. They can be used to apply a standard appearance to your web pages, as the HTML text that is to be used as a template is saved in one file, and then each individual page contains a special instruction to include this file. For example, if you want to have the same navigation bar across all your pages you could create a file called header.inc and use an SSI to include that file into each page as it is requested. It can also be used to include dynamic information in documents, such as current date, the file's last modification date, and the size or last modification of other files. SSIs are a feature of web server software.

For more information on SSIs see Server Side Includes, www.wdvl.com/Authoring/SSI/.

CGI

All web servers also come with a special CGI (common gateway interface) capability, which essentially involves the ability to run a program in a directory visible to the web server, normally called the **cgi-bin** directory. The URL of the server-side created page is something like:

www.examplewebserver.com/shopping/cgi-bin/catalogue.php

will run a program called catalogue.php which will create a web page (in this example the front page of a shopping catalogue) and return it to the user's browser. These programs are created using programming languages such as **PERL** and **PHP**.

CGI Programming 101, www.cgi101.com/book/ is the best place to start learning about CGI programming. The biggest collection of ready-made CGI scripts is the CGI Resource Index, http://cgi.resourceindex.com/.

ASP

ASP (active server pages) is a Microsoft product for building dynamic server-side web pages. All Microsoft servers Version 3 and above support the running of ASPs and it is possible for other web servers to be ASP enabled. ASP code is generally written in a language called **VBScript** and is embedded in the HTML page. When an ASP page is requested from the web server, the server first executes the ASP instructions, then constructs the page including any ASP-generated information, and returns it to the client.

For more information on how to use ASP see the ASP Tutorial for Beginners, www.asptutorial.info/.

Cookies

Server-side scripting is typically used to provide personalized content. A means of identifying a particular user/client over time is needed for this. A common way of doing this is with **cookies**. Cookies are files containing information about visitors to a website (e.g. user name and preferences). This information is stored on the user's machine in a text file during the first visit to a web server. When the user returns to the site the server can access the cookie and configure the information it shows to the user based on the cookie file. Cookies are typically used to personalize the user's experience of a site, for example it can remember the user's name and password or take the user back to the part of the site where they left off previously. They can be viewed as an invasion of privacy and users can choose to switch off the ability for their computer to accept cookie files.

> For more information about the pros and cons of using cookies in your web pages, see Cookie Central, www.cookiecentral.com/.

XML AND XSL

HTML provides a set of tags which enable data display. **Extensible markup language** (XML) provides a method of defining sets of tags which describe and structure data, but do not display it. Display is handled by style sheets.

Rather than learning tags, which you have to do to use HTML, with XML you must learn how to define tags. All tags must be self-describing, i.e. their names must describe the content they will contain. Tags must come in pairs. A pair of tags and their content is known as an **element**. Tag names can be in upper and lower case but the names in tag pairs must match, character for character and case for case. Different tag pairs may not overlap. All XML documents must follow these rules to be valid (also known as **well formed**). See the following as an example:

```
<book>
<title>Macbeth</title>
<author>
        <forename>William</forename>
        <surname>Shakespeare</surname>
</author>
</book>
```

The indentation above is not needed by XML but is used to make clear the tagging structure (also known as the **document tree**). The <'book'> tag is the **root element** of the document tree, as all other tags are enclosed by it. <'book'> is also the **parent** of <'author'> and <'title'>, as these tags are nested directly inside it. These two tags can also be described as the element content of <'book'>. Conversely, <'author'> and <'title'> can be said to be **children** (or siblings) of <'book'>. This nesting of tags can continue indefinitely: <'author'> is the parent of <'forename'> and <'surname'>, and they are its siblings. Since <'forename'> and <'surname'> have no sibling tags, they have only textual data as children, and are said to have **simple content**.

To label the above as an XML document an initial declaration is needed:

```
<?xml version="1.0"?>
```

As an alternative to using child elements to link data to an element, **attributes** can be used. An attribute is a name/value pair associated with an element. For example, to add a format to a publisher tag you can use:

```
<publisher format="paperback">Smith and
Son</publisher>
```

instead of:

```
<publisher>
<name>Smith and Son</name>
<format>paperback</format>
</publisher>
```

XML-capable browsers give a rather plain view of XML. Cascading style sheets are used to control the display of XML documents. The usage of CSS with XML is identical to that with HTML. For example:

```
book {display: block}
title {font-size:24pt; color: red}
author {font-size:16pt}
forename {color: blue}
surname {color: black}
```

will apply styles to the example given above. Note that the first style declaration (display: block) causes all the siblings of the book tag to appear on one line in the display. Also note that styles given to parent tags (author) are inherited by sibling tags. Attributes are dealt with by replacing 'attribute' by 'class' in the XML file and assigning styles in the style sheet to particular content items, for example:

```
publisher.paperback {color: yellow}
```

Like an HTML file, an XML file needs an external reference to the style sheet:

```
<?xml-stylesheet type="text/css"
href="style.css"?>
```

where style.css is the name of the external style sheet. Cascading style sheets cannot process the data within elements in any way; they only display that data. **Extensible stylesheet language** (XSL) can both allocate styles to data within elements and process the data; for example when it detects a particular element and data it can do things with the data, such as store them in a database.

XSL is more of a programming language than a style sheet definition tool.

The XML/XSL standards are maintained by the W3C. You can find details of the specifications and some useful online tutorials at the official sites: Extensible Markup Language, www.w3.org/XML/, and Extensible StyleSheet Language, www.w3.org/Style/XSL/.

XML applications and the Semantic Web

We have already covered one XML application, RSS, in Chapter 1. XML is a language for defining sets of tags, unlike HTML which is a set of tags for display of content. **Extensible hypertext markup language** (XTML), www.w3.org/TR/xhtml1/, is an XML definition of HTML, i.e. a specification of the paired tags that are allowable. For example, unlike in HTML, in XHTML tags must be paired. XML does not come with sets of tags for

There are online collections of DTDs for a wide and growing range of applications. DTD Repositories, www.xml.com/pub/rg/DTD_ Repositories, links to all of the important collections.

various applications: these sets of tags, originally called **document type definitions** (DTDs) but now known as **XML schemas**, must be worked out by a community of users and agreed by that community.

XML is the basis for the **resource description framework** (RDF), which is the language of the **Semantic Web**. The Semantic Web is the vision of Tim Berners-Lee (inventor of the web) and the W3C. The basic premise is that information in web pages is structured in such a way that machines can understand and make sense of the content.

For a fuller description of the possibilities of the Semantic Web see Tim Berners-Lee's article in the *Scientific American*, The Semantic Web: a new form of content, http://digbig.com/4bfbf.

RDF provides a set of tags for storing the meaning of terms and concepts in a form that computers can readily process. Meanings and concepts are expressed using a **metadata** format, like Dublin Core (see Chapter 10).

There are many metadata formats, some aimed at specific content types: IFLA maintains a useful list at Metadata Formats, www.ifla.org/II/metadata.htm.

As well as RDF and metadata, the Semantic Web needs **uniform resource identifiers** (URIs) which are immutable, unlike URLs, to specify entities, concepts, properties and relations between pieces of information found on the web. By describing information using RDF, metadata and URIs, it is hoped that search engines and agents will be able to make much more intelligent searches. For example, if a person searches for 'Apple' it would be possible to infer whether they are looking for information about the fruit, the record label or the computer company.

For the latest information, see the site W3C Semantic Web, www.w3.org/2001/sw/.

designing and publishing websites

INTRODUCTION

Creating pages is one thing. Organizing information upon them in a logical manner and creating paths of links between pages is quite different. Web design is a controversial field. There are no hard and fast rules. This chapter presents an approach to web design which synthesizes and simplifies a number of standard design approaches.

BASIC WEB DESIGN

Anyone can throw together a few web pages (e.g. for personal home pages). **Websites** (a homogeneous collection of interlinked web pages) are much more difficult for two reasons. First, they must incorporate a wide range of information about their subject. They may contain many hundreds of pages as a result and this raises the problem of how to organize links between all these pages. Second, websites must be fit for their purpose and serve the needs of their audience/users. This imposes constraints and demands on the website designers/maintainers.

Website design is about being able to structure information into web pages and then visualize simple navigation paths through those pages. One way of learning good website design is simply to look at other people's sites and conceptualize how they are structured. The purpose of this section is to propose and explain a checklist of features to use in appreciating good design from existing websites, so that you can design an effective website.

The main headings under which a website can be critiqued are, in order of importance:

- content
- site structure/navigation
- graphic design and page layout
- technical issues
- web presence.

These headings are covered individually, with a general comment and then an analysis of particular features to watch out for.

Content

Without content a website is useless. People will only use a website that gives them the information they need. If that information is not there they will go elsewhere. Features to check:

- Is there a particular targeted audience for this website? If so, who are they? There might be a number of different types of user in the audience.
- Does the website meet audience needs? In the content the website provides, is anything missing, or is anything repeated? Does any material look out of date or incorrect?
- Is the language used on the website too technical/too informal? Are definitions of technical jargon given? Are there grammatical slips or spelling mistakes?

- On each page is there a meaningful title, is content organized under appropriate headings, is there a clear statement of authorship, and is there a date of creation/last update?
- Is it possible to track how and when content is added to the website? Does it look as though the website could grow by adding new content over time?
- Are there warnings of unsuitable content (if necessary)?

Site structure/navigation

Content on a website must be findable by users. Content should be structured in a logical manner and links should guide a user through this content. The principle is to minimize effort on the part of the user in finding what they want. Features to check:

- Is there a main page (giving headings for all the content on a website)? Is there a site map (a graphical representation of the website)? If one of these is present, how complete, clear and concise is it?
- Are main links labelled clearly and unambiguously (e.g. not using terms like 'Miscellaneous', 'Stuff', 'Reports', etc.)? Are text links clearly described (e.g. not using phrases like 'Click here', etc.)? Are confusing icons without explanatory text used as links?
- Are there navigation aids (i.e. text/graphical navigation bars/windows giving a choice of links)? Are they used consistently in terms of their placement on the page and do they offer a sensible choice of links at all times? Is it possible to get back to the main page from any page on a website?
- Is the linking structure too 'deep' (i.e. does it take a lot of mouse clicks to get from the main page to a chosen destination page)? Can all content

on a site be found from following no more than three links starting from the main page?

- Have standard browser navigation features been interfered with? The back button should always take a user back to the previous page they viewed and text link colours should not have been changed from the default (blue=unused, red=used).
- Is there a keyword search facility? Does it find useful answers to searches?

Graphic design and page layout

The aim is to give the site an identity so that any page on it is recognizable as belonging to that site. However, this identity should not be created by overuse of graphics or brash styles. Features to check:

- Is there a consistency in the look and feel of pages? Do all pages share a common layout? Does this consistency give an interesting identity for the site?
- Has the need to scroll pages up and down and left and right been minimized?
- Have any pages been overloaded with text or graphics or both? Pages should almost never contain just text or graphics; there should always be a mixture.
- Have large and/or garish graphics been avoided? Are any graphics dull? Do all graphics serve a purpose?

Technical issues

There are many technological 'widgets' that can be used: using only those that add something to the site is the aim. Just because a technology exists does not mean it has to be used. Never assume a user possesses anything more than the most basic technology and a slow connection. Features to check:

- Does the website overstep the mark by requiring a particular browser or browser version, plug-in (extra piece of software), window size or any other technical facility from the user?
- If the website includes files that are not viewable by a web browser (e.g. Word files), does it include links to sources of free software to view those files?
- Is the speed of page loading fast enough (i.e. does the site avoid using overlarge graphic files, complex pages, etc.)? Is a 'text only' version of the website available (these can offset speed problems)?
- Do any pages contain broken links, missing graphics or generate browser errors?

Web presence

A website needs to be in portals and search engines on the internet if people are to know of its existence. It must state a privacy policy with regard to gathering data on users and it must give contact details (including standard address information). Features to check:

- Is the website findable in major search engines/subject listings (e.g. AskJeeves, Google, Yahoo!, Dmoz, etc.)?
- Does the website state its privacy policy (i.e. how it records visitor information and what it does with that information)?
- Does the website provide adequate contact information (address/telephone/fax) and an e-mail address for questions, comments, etc.?
- Has the website won any awards? Does it offer any usage statistics

(how many pages are accessed or how many unique users visit over a period of time) to show how popular it is?

The purpose of website critiquing is to develop skills in looking at other people's sites and conceptualizing how they are structured. It is a vital first step in website design. Whereas website design critiquing is reactive, website design implementation skills are proactive, enabling the creation of a new site rather than the examination of an existing one. There are no shortcuts to success. Software tools (such as WYSIWYG page creation tools) can only serve someone who understands how to design. In themselves they give no help with the design process whatsoever. Design is a conceptual process, not a mechanical one.

STAGES OF WEBSITE DESIGN

Whatever tool you use, a website design breaks down into four stages:

- identification of user groups
- content ordering/labelling
- structuring content
- enabling navigation.

Each of these stages is considered below.

Identification of user groups

The audience for a website could be made of many distinct groups. Each group has particular needs which must be met by the provision of certain content. Some needs, and thus content, might be shared by different groups. By far the best way of determining user needs is to ask users what they want. Failing the availability of users, a designer can create a table listing 'Audience' against 'Needs' and then 'Content required' to satisfy needs.

Content ordering/labelling

Content ordering is concerned with how individual pieces of content are to be grouped together. Some sort of logical ordering is needed. There are two basic ways of approaching content, each requiring different ordering schemes:

- **known item search** – when users know exactly what they want
- **browse search** – when users have only a vague feeling about what they want.

Known item searches are best aided by alphabetical, chronological, numeric or geographical orderings. Conversely, browse searches are best supported by subject/topic/type or task-oriented orderings. The latter are the hardest orderings to construct as all members of a subject/topic/type/ task must be explicitly defined. Consult dictionaries and thesauri to derive complete lists of members. Care must be taken to label each member as clearly and unambiguously as possible. Labels should be consistent, e.g. using plural forms where possible. Most websites will be hybrid, containing mixtures of orderings.

Structuring content

Once content orderings are known, it is possible to derive a web structure from them. Most websites have hierarchical structures, starting from a **home/main/index/top page**. From this page there should be a limited number of choices which lead down to pages on the second level of the hierarchy. These choices will be based on the content orderings and labels derived earlier. Very often there will be a plethora of possible choices/links to put on the home page. The way around this problem is to make choices on the home page related to used types. Then each specific user type can be given a reduced but appropriate set of content choices.

According to research into how people interact with web pages, the number of choices (in terms of different links to follow) given to a user in any one page should not be more than seven. However, research has also shown that people soon give up rather than follow a long path of links to get to the content they want. To resolve this problem, many sites (e.g. Yahoo!) present users with many choices on the home page to lead them straight down to a page on the next level that has the content that they want.

Enabling navigation

Navigation enables a user to plan a route, to determine their current location and to move up and down the hierarchy, as well as follow related paths between different sections of the hierarchy. Once content ordering has been done, and a hierarchy derived, navigation aids can be produced. Basic navigations aids on each page might be:

- a consistently placed **menu** of links to other pages
- a **path** showing the titles of pages visited previously.

Extra navigation aids include:

- a **table of contents page**
- an **index page** (like a book index)
- a **site map** (a picture of the hierarchy)
- a **guided tour**.

Website design is an art not a science. Some sites deliberately break the rules suggested above and still manage to be successful! However, it is not advisable to break rules until they have been learned and understood. It is vital to test any prototype website on representative users from audience groups you have identified. Take their comments on board and keep iteratively redesigning your website and retesting it with users until they give it the all-clear.

There are plenty of sources of design advice. Jacob Nielsen is a respected web design guru: his AlertBox, www.useit.com/alertbox/, is always a source of solid advice. Web Pages that Suck, www.webpagesthatsuck.com/, is an amusing collection of examples to avoid, not follow. The Web Style Guide, www.webstyleguide.com/, is a well respected manual that many follow. Finally, Style and Design, http://directory.google.com/Top/Computers/Internet/Web_Design_and_Development/Authoring/Style_and_Design/?il=1, contains an enormous collection of links to website design resources.

PUBLISHING A WEBSITE

Creating a website is only the first stage to publishing it on the world wide web. When you have finished designing your website it will be stored on your own (or another local machine) and will be visible only via the web browser on that machine. Publishing a website basically involves moving all the files in your website onto a **web server** (a software program that sends out web pages in response to browser requests).

Web servers

But before you do this there is a vital stage to go through first! This is checking. Check your pages for spelling and grammatical errors before publishing them. Check that all the images you are using display properly in your browser. You must also check that your HTML is correct and that all links work.

The W3C Markup Validation Service, http://validator.w3.org/, and the W3C Link Checker, http://validator.w3.org/checklink, will check your HTML and links.

Your pages can go on either your own server or one owned by someone else. You may have a server already and not know it. Most computer operating systems these days come with a basic web server.

For example, Installing Internet Information Server on Windows XP, www.webwizguide.com/asp/tutorials/installing_iis_winXP_pro.asp, shows you how to set up the web server that comes with Windows XP.

If your users are all going to be on the same local network as your machine then this type of web server might be sufficient. The only drawback is that a web server running on your machine will take up your machine's resources and you might find other functions start to slow down!

Typically another machine in your organization will be designated as running a web server, so your web pages need to be copied onto that machine. Your network may have a special facility for transferring files. WYSIWYG page creation tools usually have file copying facilities included. Finally, if all else fails, **FTP** (file transfer protocol) software (see Chapter 4) will do the job.

Web hosting

If you or your organization have no web server you must use an external web server via a **web hosting service** (a company running web servers for others' use). For personal use a free web hosting service is ideal.

Free Hosting, http://directory.google.com/Top/ Computers/Internet/Web_Design_ and_Development/Hosting/Free/, gives a list of free providers.

While they are free the main drawbacks of such services are the limits they impose on the volume of files they will store and the amount of **traffic** (usage in terms of being requested and sent out via the internet). For serious web hosting you need a commercial web hosting service.

There are three basic types of hosting packages:

- **virtual** – your website is stored somewhere on a server farm (group of computers acting as one web server) at the commercial web host
- **dedicated** – your website is stored on a particular machine at the commercial web host
- **collocated** – your website is stored on a particular machine at your premises but maintained by people from the commercial web host.

Virtual hosting is the cheapest option, and normally the one chosen. Dedicated and collocated hosting are more expensive but give you greater control and reliability, and possibly a faster response for users.

The wise purchaser of any sort of hosting package should consider:

- How much web space is offered? (the more the better)
- How fast is the internet connection? (the faster the better)
- Can it offer and register a recognizable URL? (e.g. www.yourname.com)
- What support does it offer? (i.e. phone lines, e-mail, conferencing, etc.)
- Does it offer CGI, ASP, server-side scripting? (if you need this facility).

Problems with web hosting packages to watch out for are:

- **resellers** – these are people selling on web space they have bought from other web hosting services. This is potentially bad because you are not dealing with the real owner of the web host. Problems may go unsolved, etc.
- **bandwidth restrictions** (i.e. a limit on the amount of traffic your website can generate) – all web hosting services have a limited (in terms of traffic capability) internet connection. Typically, if your website

generates more than the expected traffic you might be charged extra or your site shut down and moved to more expensive hosting.

- **downtime and responsiveness** (i.e. is the hosting web server ever not functioning or responding very slowly to browser requests?) – try accessing a website you know is running on a potential commercial web host over a period of time. Does it always respond quickly? Is it ever down?

Choosing a commercial web hosting service is very difficult. However, there are plenty of commercial hosts so there is no reason to stay with one for ever.

United Kingdom Web Hosting Directories, http://directory.google.com/Top/Regional/Europe/United_Kingdom/Business_and_Economy/Computers _andInternet/Internet/Web_Hosting/Directories/, gives a listing of advice and review sites for commercial web hosting and directory access to a large number of hosts.

Website promotion

Once a website is operational, people will not find it unless they come across its URL. Traditional means of promotion (e.g. putting a URL on all literature/letterheads, etc.) should be used but successfully promoting a website essentially involves getting it recognized, and indexed, by the major search engines. If this is not done then a website will not get visitors.

Most search engines have some method of submission. There are services that can send a registration automatically to a range of search engines at the same time. See the sites listed at Promotion: Submissions, http://directory.google.com/Top/Computers/Internet/Web_Design_and_Development/ Promotion/Tools/Submissions/.

However, merely submitting the URL of your website's home page is not enough. You must consider how words and phrases in that page will be chosen by search engines to index your page. Typically search engines will index words/phrases in the page title (between the <TITLE> headers), headers on the page (between <H> tags), the initial paragraphs and **meta tags** in the page header, specifically content following the 'subject' and 'keywords' attributes, for example:

```
<HEAD>
<META NAME="DESCRIPTION "CONTENT="A statement of your
website's subject coverage">
<META NAME="KEYWORDS" CONTENT="keyword 1, keyword 2
etc">
</HEAD>
```

Note that meta tags are a primitive precursor of the RDF-tagged metadata discussed previously. Their content is not seen by someone looking at your web page, but it can be picked by internet search engines. The description attribute is important because you can include a short paragraph about your site, or service: some search engines will display this in their search results. Many search engines do not index the keywords attribute any more but you can use this to come up with synonyms of terms that don't appear in your site. You can add Dublin Core (or some other scheme) metadata to your web pages but as this is not supported by search engines it is normally used as a means of improving internal indexing and searching.

Another useful meta tag is the **robots** attribute, which allows you to specify if you don't want your site to be indexed by search engines. There

The HTML Author's Guide to the Robots META tag site, www.robotstxt.org/wc/meta-user.html, gives advice on how to deploy this facility. Alternatively, you could include a robots.txt file in your server to specify precisely which parts of the website may be indexed. The Robots.txt Tutorial, www.searchengineworld.com/robots/robots_tutorial.htm, shows how this file is used.

might be good reasons for this: your website might be under development, or frequently overloaded with requests.

Finally, be careful about the contents of the <TITLE> tag: it is also the default title if a user chooses to store it in their 'favourites' or 'bookmarks' so try to make it as informative and specific as possible. The suggestions given about how search engines index content are very general. Search engines differ in how they index and exactly how they index is normally a closely guarded commercial secret.

> The Promotions – FAQs, Help and Tutorials site,
> http://directory.google.com/Top/Computers/Internet/Web_Design_and_Development/Promotion/FAQs,
> _Help,_and_Tutorials/?il=1, links to many sources of advice on **search rankings** (i.e. how to help your
> website rank higher in particular searches).

> Of course, **paid listings** (i.e. adverts) on search engines are a possible way of promoting your website!

Link exchange schemes (making reciprocal links between websites) and **web rings** (directly linking sites on a common theme) can also be used. Be careful to pick appropriate link exchange schemes as some are scams.

> For advice, see Reciprocal Links,
> http://directory.google.com/Top/Computers/Internet/Web_Design_and_Development/Promotion/
> Link_Popularity/Reciprocal_Links/, and WebRing, http://dir.webring.com/rw.

Finally, do not forget that sites can also be promoted by posting their details to appropriate mailing lists and newsgroups (see Chapters 5 and 6 for more information on these).

Usage tracking

Once a website has been promoted/announced then **usage tracking** needs to take place. This means knowing who is looking at what pages and when, and maybe even recording a user's entire path through a site and possibly their past usage history. There are various means of tracking usage, from the simple to the sophisticated.

The simplest method is to solicit feedback from users by means of **mailto** links (links which open an e-mailer with a send window to a particular e-mail address) and HTML **forms** (web pages customized to allow the input of responses and structured data). This can be an effective way of getting user comments. A mailto link might be:

```
<A HREF="mailto:someone@someorganisation.
co.uk"> Click here to email us your
comments></A>
```

Forms are very easy to design in HTML and a server-side script can be used to collect user responses and store them in a file ready for analysis.

The Forms site, http://webreference.com/ programming/forms.html, has a collection of tutorials on forms.

The simplest quantitative method is to use a **page counter**, an application that counts page accesses.

There is a collection of page counters at Counters and Trackers, http://directory.google.com/Top/Computers/Internet/Web_Design_and_Development/Hosted_ Components_and_Services/Counters_and_Trackers/.

However, page accesses on their own tell very little, apart from revealing that a page is getting usage. Most professional websites use **log analysis** software which reveals a whole lot more. All web server software logs (creates a record of) the pages sent out and the internet destinations of those pages.

The Log Analysis,
http://directory.google.com/Top/Computers/Software/Internet/Site_Management/Log_Analysis/,
maintains a list of log analyser tools: some are free.

You might want to compare your website's usage against those of comparable sites.

Alexa, www.alexa.com, maintains a database of websites ordered in terms of their usage as tracked by Alexa. You can search for a website to see its usage details.

Finally, cookies (see Chapter 2) can be used to track users. This involves storing site-specific information in a file called cookies.txt on a user's computer.

Whatever method (or methods) of usage tracking you use, beware of infringing users' rights to privacy. A website should always declare any usage tracking features. There is a standard method of doing this, see the Platform for Privacy Preferences, www.w3.org/P3P/.

ADVANCED WEBSITE MANAGEMENT

It is actually very easy to create and publish a website. However, the vast majority of websites, once published, are never updated! Thus their usefulness is extremely limited, and after a while they atrophy. When setting up a website make sure you plan for the continual addition of new, relevant content over time.

Getting content onto a website can be a major hurdle. People publish content in all sorts of formats. Translating these formats (e.g. Word) straight into HTML is not a good idea as the end-products simply will not conform to the standard design set for a particular website. Content will also come from a variety of people: some of them will not want to do anything at all to get their content on the website, and others will want to put that content there themselves and maintain it themselves. Both types of person cause problems. Typically a bottleneck develops with the harassed website maintainer trying to obtain content from reluctant individuals while fighting off demands for rights for everyone to mount content on the website.

Content management

To cope with these demands for continual change in content and 'self-service authoring', whereby content creators do not need to be skilled in the use of technical tools (e.g. web editors) some form of automated support is needed. **Content management systems** (CMS) are one means of providing this automated support and of ensuring the longevity of content in the web environment.

However, a content management system is not an off-the-shelf unitary product, but rather a set of management processes and software tools. Since organizational needs, processes and existing information systems will vary, a one-size-fits-all CMS is impossible, making the implementation of a CMS an art more than a science. Since factors change over time, implementation can be a continual task, rather than a discrete event. CMS functions overlap closely with document management systems, knowledge management systems and web-publishing systems, and more loosely with portals, groupware and even virtual learning environments.

The functions of a CMS are to enable the input and editing of content, to integrate diverse content (e.g. in different formats), to republish that content in different formats and on different technical platforms (e.g. web, mobile phones), and to manage content over time, using metadata which describes the value and purpose of content. These functions can be illustrated by the following example of publishing a library guide:

EXAMPLE: PUBLISHING A LIBRARY GUIDE

Integrating content from diverse sources – content comes from staff, photographers and specialists like systems personnel, in a variety of formats.

Publishing the same content in different formats – the library guide could be printed, viewed as a web page, appear in large-print for a partially sighted user, etc.

Accepting content from many creators while enabling the editorial control of a few – many departments and individuals could contribute to the guide but significant interests (the Head of the Library, etc.) would need to vet and approve material.

Enabling the sophisticated presentation of content from a simple means of creating that content – an individual could fill in a simple form (e.g. for end-of-year finances) which would give that content an appropriate location and appearance in the guide.

Adding appropriate metadata (e.g. time/date of creation, name of creator, subject, etc.) to content to facilitate its management – the printed guide has appropriate captions and credits for pictures, the online version has keywords appropriate for search engine indexing, etc.

Storing content for retrieval and reuse in the future – past copies of the guide both printed and online could be used later in an exhibit of the library's history, etc.

For a definitive list of CMS products, refer to Content Management, http://directory.google.com/Top/Computers/Software/Internet/Site_Management/ Content_Management/.

Accessibility

A facility of CMS is the ability to publish the same content in different formats. Even if you are not using a CMS you must address this issue. Any web material should be **accessible** (in terms of readability) to the widest possible audience. Web pages must work for people who cannot see graphical content. There is specific pressure from the new Disability Discrimination Act to improve websites. Part 4 of the Act makes it a requirement that public sector websites are accessible to all. This is not an onerous extra task as making a site accessible – this primarily means for the visually impaired – tends to be good for all users. A minimum requirement is to provide advice on accessibility, such as on increasing the size of type within a browser and to use <ALT> tags (textual alternatives to pictures and images that can be read out by a **screen-reader**, software which converts text to speech), for example:

```
<img src="pictureofthelibrary.gif" alt="A
picture of the front of the library, showing
the main doors and wheelchair ramp and the
main service desk behind">
```

For information on creating websites accessible by those with visual disabilities, see AbilityNet, www.abilitynet.org.uk/, the RNIB's Web Access Centre, www.rnib.org.uk/xpedio/groups/public/documents/PublicWebsite/public_webaccesscentre.hcsp, and the Web Accessibility Initiative's Getting Started: Making a Website Accessible, www.w3.org/WAI/gettingstarted/. An invaluable tool which checks a website for its accessibility is WebXACT, http://webxact.watchfire.com/.

file transfer technologies

INTRODUCTION

Transferring files is an essential element of the internet. We have already covered the transfer of files via the world wide web such as clicking links to load files in your web browser, uploading web pages to a server and downloading software, but there are other ways to transfer files on the internet. The ability of users to e-mail a file to a colleague or friend is an example of day-to-day transfer of files.

FILE TRANSFER PROTOCOL (FTP)

File transfer protocol, more commonly referred to as FTP, is one of the oldest file transfer tools on the internet. FTP involves transferring a file either from your machine to a server or from the server to your own computer. You might use FTP to move files around your local network or to publish files on a web server. FTP can also be used to retrieve files on the internet.

The best searching tool is FileSearching.com, www.filesearching.com/.

To use FTP you need a **client** version of an FTP program, or you can use a web browser (although dedicated FTP software programs are more reliable if you are transferring lots of files).

A variety of FTP clients is available from Download.com's directory FTP, www.download.com/FTP/ 3150-2160_4-0.html?tag=dir.

Transferring files from a remote site

To start an FTP transfer, you first give the host and domain name of the site to which you want to connect (see Chapter 8 for more on host/domain names). At the login prompt from the remote site, you enter anonymous. This is the standard response for **anonymous FTP** which allows anyone to log in. Enter your own e-mail address at the password prompt which appears next. This is purely a courtesy, so that the operators of an FTP service know who has used it. Finally, you will see a display of a part of the site's file system, containing files for transfer. See Chapter 1 for more on files and file systems.

There are a few things to remember, whatever type of client you are using for FTP:

- Do be aware of the size of the file (or files) you are wishing to transfer. The problem here is very large files, which can take a while to transfer. Your FTP client should be able to show you file sizes.
- FTP sites are essentially collections of files, just like the collection of files on your own computer, and sometimes exploring directories in an FTP site might find other files, which from their names might appear to be of interest to you.
- When you finish your FTP transfers you should **close** (i.e. terminate the FTP connection) properly. Leaving old connections active can waste network resources.

Transferring files to a remote site

FTP can also be used to transfer files to, rather than from, a remote site. This is known as **uploading**. For security reasons many sites do not allow this. Those sites that do usually have a directory called **incoming** to receive files. Uploaded files should be accompanied by a description of their contents and the uploader's name and e-mail address. If considered suitable for the collection at the remote FTP site, uploaded files will be transferred to an appropriate directory. If not, they will almost certainly be deleted.

Text and non-text files

Computer files fall into two types: text files and non-text (**binary**) files. Plain text files contain only characters from the **ASCII** (American Standard Code for Information Interchange, and pronounced *Ass-key*) character set, which is used by all computers. Thus they can be stored, displayed and printed on any computer and are reasonably easy to transfer from one computer to another. You can transfer non-text files using anonymous FTP but you might have to make your client aware that transfers will be of binary files, rather than ASCII files. FTP clients usually default to ASCII transfers. Transferring a file in the wrong mode will render it useless.

How do you know whether a file contains just text or not? It is impossible to say from a file name whether the file is a text file or a non-text file. There are **conventions** for filename extensions (i.e. the final three characters of the filename) which indicate file format (e.g. 'txt' for text files) but these conventions can be ignored. If you are using a graphical client, the type of file may be indicated by a suitable icon, but really the only definitive test is to transfer a file and then view it with a text editor. If it contains ordinary characters from beginning to end then it is a text file; if it is unreadable or contains unusual characters then it is probably a non-text file. 'Readme' files can be considered to contain text.

In order to save space on FTP sites, non-text files are usually compressed. For more on file compression, see Chapter 1.

PEER-TO-PEER FILE TRANSFER (P2P)

Peer-to-peer file sharing, or P2P as it is more commonly known, involves two or more users on a network sharing files directly from their computers rather than using a server as intermediary. This model is growing more and more as broadband internet access becomes more common. Rather than having a dial-up connection to an ISP, broadband allows a computer to be online all the time, meaning files can be shared from a computer hard drive at any time, even when the owner of the computer is not there. See Chapter 8 for more information.

Software is available on the web to enable surfers to share their files across the internet, perhaps the most infamous being the original Napster, www.napster.co.uk/, now reborn as a legal commercial music download service.

> Kazaa, www.kazaa.com/, is one of a large number of P2P packages: the File Sharing site, http://directory.google.com/Top/Computers/Software/Internet/Clients/File_Sharing/, has an exhaustive listing. The number of P2P packages stems from a variety of methods of operation and transfer capability. For example, BitTorrent, http://bittorrent.com/, specializes in extremely large files while the Freenet Project, www.freenetproject.org/, offers a client which keeps users anonymous and encrypts (scrambles) files stored so that what is stored there is also hidden.

The main characteristic of all current P2P packages is that they create a **decentralized** network, that is one in which no one machine stores a record of the location of every file. The original Napster was **centralized**, i.e. it maintained a single database which recorded the location of all shared files. It was this mode of operation which caused its legal downfall for copyright infringement because it could be targeted.

When it was shut down in 2001, Napster contained millions of music tracks, most of them copyrighted. It also contained books (in a variety of file formats) and images (many of which were pornographic). It even contained some television programmes and films but the sheer size of these files made them extremely slow and cumbersome to download. But music tracks were the most popular: they were reasonably swift to download, especially through broadband connections. The file format responsible for this was **MPEG3** (usually given as MP3) which stored music files in a compressed form. **Ripping** (copying tracks in CD audio format) onto a computer, and then **burning** (converting those tracks into MP3 format and storing them onto writeable CDs) produced CDs carrying ten times as much music as before.

The current Napster, and other legal music download services, offer music tracks but in formats other than MP3, such as Microsoft's **Windows Media Audio** (WMA) and Apple's **Advanced Audio Coding** (AAC). That is because these formats include **digital rights management** (DRM) features which restrict the playing of tracks to the individual who purchases them and the devices on which they will play.

Pro-Music, www.pro-music.org/musiconline.htm, is a directory of legal music download services.

Copyright

P2P file sharing has become one of the most controversial issues with regards the internet. The issue of file sharing **copyright materials** is one that is rarely out of the professional computing and internet press:

> [In] the digital music era and the dawn of the Internet and 'file-sharing', technological advances have allowed the art of sharing to evolve from localized to global exchanges. One can now 'share' software

and music products with others around the world, without even knowing with whom one is sharing. Furthermore, one can share exponentially – a single original good file generating thousands or millions of reproductions. The global expansion of illegal sharing, common among software and music products, has become a critical problem threatening the value of intellectual property.

(Chiang and Assane, 2002, 145)

While the popularity of such services is beyond doubt, they offer major challenges for information professionals both in terms of legal access to information, and in terms of managing the ICT infrastructure of their organization.

It can be easy to take the side of the individual in this and say that file sharing does not harm the production of intellectual property. Indeed one of the core roles of the profession could be under threat as new information professionals qualify who see no real issues in terms of illegal file sharing. As Rupp and Smith have suggested:

It has become a norm to download music off the Internet and transfer it onto compact discs (CD) without compensating the artist who created the music or the firms that created, packaged, promoted, and distributed the music materials. Few if any people think twice that they are breaking the law by making a copy of material to which they do not own the copyrights. Piracy . . . is rampant and routinely practiced throughout the world.   (Rupp and Smith, 2004, 103)

The new Code of Practice adopted by the Chartered Institute of Library and Information Professionals (CILIP) states that it is the ethical duty of a member to:

> Defend the legitimate needs and interests of information users, while
> upholding the moral and legal rights of the creators and distributors
> of intellectual property.   (CILIP, 2004)

And certainly it is difficult to argue that file sharing of copyrighted materials, despite the fashion towards this, should be supported by information professionals in this context.

In March 2004 rights-holders began a high-profile campaign in Europe, following on from an earlier equally high-profile campaign in the USA, to bring to court individuals they claimed had offered thousands of copyrighted files free to be downloaded on the internet. The campaign targeted 247 people across continental Europe in countries where the record industry claimed that CD sales had fallen as a result of illegal sharing of music. Despite a recent study by two American researchers (Oberholzer and Strumpf, 2004), suggesting that music downloading was statistically insignificant in terms of its impact on CD sales, record companies are adamant that file sharing is impacting greatly on their income, and, crucially, they are determined to do what they can about it through the legal system.

Whether one agrees with the rights-holders in their quest to make it harder to file share, the age-old and vital role of the information professional in protecting intellectual property rights, while at the same time providing access, is greatly challenged by the exponential growth of P2P file sharing. As an issue this will grow in importance, and there is always the danger that information organizations in the business of providing public access to the internet could become a target as customers who use public facilities to break copyright laws become a focus for rights-holders. In the context of internet service providers (ISPs) Conradi suggests that rigorous **acceptable use policies** (AUPs) can shield the organization from much of the responsibility and pass the liability to the user where it technically belongs. However, he acknowledges that there can never be a 100% guarantee that legal claims against the organization providing internet access would fail, should a rights-holder decide to lodge such an action (Conradi, 2003, 289). He also highlights the 2003 ruling against easyinternetcafe where it was found to be in breach of copyright law by allowing users to download music and burn the files onto CD on its premises. After a protracted legal dispute, easyinternetcafe settled the case by paying the British phonographic industry £80,000 plus legal fees of £130,000. This case highlights the potential dangers in being unaware of users using library computers to burn material onto CD. Unless you are 100% sure about your security, it can be difficult to know if a user is doing what eventually cost easyinternetcafe £210,000.

ALTERNATIVE SYSTEMS TO PROTECT INTELLECTUAL PROPERTY

Copyright law has its challengers, not those who download music illegally, but those who try to propose alternative systems for the protection of intellectual property.

Creative Commons, http://creativecommons.org/, is a clearing house of projects and ideas that try to strike new balances between content producers and content consumers. The Electronic Frontier Foundation's (EFF) Intellectual Property page, www.eff.org/IP/, details current copyright lawsuits in a wide range of domains, as well as cases that the EFF itself is involved in. Stanford University Libraries Copyright and Fair Use Center, http://fairuse.stanford.edu/, is also a useful clearinghouse, with specific resources angled towards librarians. What is Copyleft?, www.gnu.org/copyleft/copyleft.html, and the Open Source Initiative, www.opensource.org/, propose systems for the free (but with rights and responsibilities) distribution of software. Finally, Brendan Scott's Copyright in a Frictionless World, www.firstmonday.org/issues/issue6_9/scott/, is a stimulating and coherent challenge to current copyright law.

SPYWARE AND ADWARE

Spyware and adware are increasingly annoying to internet users
worldwide. Both types of program can be spread by file sharing systems
such as Kazaa: when loading this software you also install several spyware
and adware programs to your system. In addition they can be spread when
visitors to websites have to load a hijacked plug-in or extra program to
their web browser to view specific content.

Spyware

Spyware programs, once installed on to your system, gather information
about your surfing habits and transmit this information back to a company
or organization that finances the software. This is normally undertaken for
marketing reasons, building a picture of surfing habits in order to target you
with specific marketing material. The development of spyware has been a
direct result of the fashion to obtain things free from the internet; spyware
essentially pays for services such as Kazaa to exist, as marketers pay Kazaa
to supply their spyware with every download of their file-sharing software.
As well as P2P file sharing software, spyware can also be attached to other
types of free software you may get on the internet. The justification is again
that since you are obtaining free software, the programmer has a right to
pay for their intellectual property by attaching spyware. As Klang has stated:

> The creators of the downloaded software claim that their actions are
> both legal and driven from economic necessity. Users demand free
> software, software manufacturers need funding to create more
> competitive software and marketers need to reach potential
> customers. Since the users obtain free software, software houses
> obtain a new source of income and the marketers increase their
> reach. (Klang, 2003, 314)

The annoyance aspect of spyware aside, there are serious data protection and privacy issues that should be of concern to information professionals. While the legal defence of spyware providers that users who download the software are aware of the privacy issues by agreeing to the licence when they install the software is technically correct, the truth is that many users do not bother to read licence agreements on software. While this is not a defence in a court of law, it remains the case that many users are completely unaware of what the spyware is doing and what information on their surfing habits is being communicated.

Adware

Adware is software that is installed in a similar way to spyware and is designed to deliver advertisements to your desktop. While the program is running on your computer it pulls down adverts from the internet and as such is communicating with a server to do so. Again this usually means that your computer is communicating with another computer without your knowledge, and this has serious issues with regards privacy.

Bandwidth wastage

Another important issue to consider with regards spyware and adware is the waste of resources they can facilitate. The bandwidth of an organization can be impacted greatly by spyware and adware consistently sending data across the internet. If an organization has a number of computers all infected by such software there is a real possibility that bandwidth, which costs money, is being wasted by the software. As an example, if the spyware or adware is old, and the servers they use to communicate have closed for whatever reason, the software may still continue to attempt to communicate. Not receiving a signal, it may attempt to do so continuously, causing system resources on the computer to be impacted as well as the bandwidth of the organization. If this happens it is rare that anything visible is going on in front of your eyes; your computer may appear slower than normal, but there will be nothing obvious.

Software is available that can identify if your computer has been infected by spyware or adware, and it is wise to check occasionally if you have been infected by such programs.

Download.com's Spyware Center, www.download.com/Spyware-Center/2001-2023_4-0.html?tag=dir, offers practical advice and links to a range of spyware and adware removal tools.

Similar to spyware, **cookies** are files that are stored on your computer containing information on your internet surfing. Cookies have been covered in Chapter 2. Unlike spyware they do not build a picture of what you are doing while online but instead store information related to your use of a specific website, for instance things like usernames or passwords. There is a debate about whether cookies can also be considered as spyware because they do contain information that is specific to the user. However, cookies are normally only storing information relevant to a specific website and your visits to it. Again, the issues of data protection and privacy are of relevance in the debate. On a positive note, cookies can be disabled within web browsers using the preferences option; therefore the user has more control over these types of files than they do over spyware or adware.

It is important for information professionals to keep up to date with issues regarding spyware and the like. Previously issues that were of interest only to systems and support staff, they can have such a negative impact on service delivery in the digital library that awareness is crucial. To use an analogy, if a collection of books were in danger of being damaged via water seepage or mites, the correct reaction would be to protect the resources with the safeguards at your disposal. In the digital era, protection of computers and internet bandwidth are as crucial if service levels are to remain at the highest levels.

REFERENCES

Chiang, E. and Assane, D. (2002) Copyright Piracy on the University Campus: trends and lessons from the software and music industries, *International Journal on Media Management*, 4 (3), 145–9.

CILIP (2004) *Ethical Principles and Code of Professional Practice for Library and Information Professionals*, www.cilip.org.uk/professionalguidance/ethics/.

Conradi, M. (2003) Liability of an ISP for Allowing Access to File Sharing Networks, *Computer Law & Security Report*, 19 (4), 289–94.

Klang, M. (2003) Spyware: paying for software with our privacy, *International Review of Law, Computers and Technology*, 17 (3), (November), 313–22.

Oberholzer, F. and Strumpf, K. (2004*) The Effect of File Sharing on Record Sales: an empirical analysis*, University of North Carolina, www.unc.edu/~cigar/papers/FileSharing_March2004.pdf.

Rupp, W. T. and Smith, A. D. (2004) Exploring the Impacts of P2P Networks on the Entertainment Industry, *Information Management & Computer Security*, 12 (1), 102–16.

INTRODUCTION

Fundamentally, the internet provides access to people and to information resources (i.e. files). The latter have been covered in Chapters 1 and 4. In this chapter the topic is how to contact people on the internet.

It is virtually impossible to monitor how many people have internet access. Some potential users never actually use their internet connection. Other people have a number of different internet connections. However, estimates suggest that just over 600 million people currently have access to the internet: see the site NUA Internet: How Many Online, www.nua.ie/surveys/how_many_online/. The turnover of users on some sites (e.g. at universities, when student cohorts change annually) is large. In the UK (as in most countries outside the USA) the majority of users in the early days of the internet were members of the academic community, but the mid-1990s saw a huge number of non-academic institutions join the internet, following the trend in the USA where the internet had for several years been widely used by people in industry, commerce and government and by private citizens.

Essentially there are three ways of communicating with other internet users:

- electronic mail (e-mail)
- electronic conferencing systems
- 'live' interactive systems where the participants are connected simultaneously.

Electronic mail is used by individuals or groups to pass messages between each other and is available to virtually the whole internet community. Conferencing systems allow people to contribute to a central pool of discussion on a topic; others can then selectively pick up and respond to individual messages in the pool. Live, interactive systems are used to communicate in 'real time'; in effect, participants are 'talking' rather than passing messages between each other. This chapter concentrates on e-mail. See Chapters 6 and 7 for the other ways of communicating with people.

ELECTRONIC MAIL

E-mails are text messages sent between individuals on the internet. Sending an e-mail involves composing a text message and sending it to an individual whose e-mail address is known. A subject, which summarizes the message, is also normally added. Records of an individual's sent and received e-mails are normally kept and can be reviewed to track conversations.

Addresses

E-mail provides a fast, cheap and convenient means of passing messages between individuals and groups. For many users it is the first internet application they come into contact with and remains the most important. On the internet, an **e-mail address** is made up of three elements:

- a user identifier
- a separator character – @

- a host/domain name (see Chapter 8 for more on host/domain names).

Examples are:

- A.J.Smith@someuniversity.ac.uk
- enquiry-desk@somepubliclibrary.org.uk

Incoming messages go into a file called a mailbox on the computer identified by the host and domain name. Usually a user has their own personal mailbox, although it is possible to have a shared mailbox with other users (sales and customer support departments often do this, as in the enquiry-desk example above). A user identifier can be any combination of letters and numbers: it is useful to have a user identifier related to your name (e.g. initials followed by surname). Some sites with many users avoid name clashes by adding numbers to the user identifier (e.g. Jane Smith is J.Smith1, John Smith is J.Smith2, etc.).

It is usually straightforward to find the e-mail address of someone at your own site. It can be a bigger problem to find an address for someone at a different site. No universal directories of e-mail addresses exist. There are too many e-mail users each with one or more addresses. Not surprisingly the directories that do exist are incomplete.

Recommendations for directories to try are InfoSpace, www.infospace.com, Yahoo! People Search, http://people.yahoo.com, and People Search, www.addresses.com.

You can use standard search tools to search for a person's name, hoping to find a page with their e-mail address. If you know where the person works, try their organization's website because it might include a searchable directory of employees. If all else fails, ring the person and ask them for their e-mail address!

E-mailer clients

E-mail appears to the recipient as a list of messages from their mailbox presented by an **e-mailer** (client software for handling e-mail). The display of the messages is determined by the e-mailer you use. A range of clients is available, and some are included in other packages (e.g. Outlook comes with Windows).

Download.com has a collection of e-mailers at E-mail Software, www.download.com/E-mail/ 2001-2158_4-0.html?tag=dir.

The elements of a typical e-mail include at least:

- the sender's name (and/or their e-mail address)
- a subject
- the date and time sent
- the actual message.

The order of messages is controlled by the e-mailer. The user can usually specify whether messages are ordered by date of arrival, subject, name of sender or message size. All e-mailers allow messages to be read on screen, and printed if necessary. When you read an e-mail message you will see at the top a **header**. This consists of the sender and recipient's e-mail addresses, the subject, the date and time of sending and routing information (how the e-mail reached your machine). The message itself follows the header. Some e-mailers have facilities for searching for a particular message (e.g. by sender's name), or for searching within a message for a word.

All e-mailers allow you to delete messages or to save them in named **folders**. A folder is a file of e-mail just like your mailbox, but which you can name in a meaningful way, to enable you to find the e-mail again later.

Your e-mailer will allow you to switch to one of these folders to read stored e-mail. It is good practice to clear your incoming mailbox each time you use it.

Web mail

You may want **remote access** to your e-mail, e.g. while at home or on holiday abroad. **Web mail** is a method of reading your e-mail via a web page: essentially this web page acts like your e-mail package. Most organizations now provide this mode of access to e-mail. If your organization does not then it is possible to create an e-mail account for yourself on a free **internet web mail service** and set your e-mail account to **forward** e-mail there. Note that your organization might not want you to do this if your e-mail is likely to contain confidential information. Many people have at least one internet web mail account as well as their professional e-mail address.

> There are many web mail services: see Free Web-Based E-Mail,
> http://directory.google.com/Top/Computers/Internet/E-mail/Free/Web-Based/, for a listing of hundreds!
> Popular choices are Hotmail, www.hotmail.com, and Yahoo! Mail, http://mail.yahoo.com/.

Increasingly internet web mail services do not require you to forward e-mail to them but can be configured (if you know the appropriate technical details) to access e-mail from **post office protocol** (POP) or **internet message access protocol** (IMAP) accounts.

Features of e-mail

Signatures

Some people end their e-mail messages with a **signature**, a few lines that say who they are, where they work and give contact information such as telephone and fax numbers, as well as their e-mail address. Sometimes signatures contain a witty quote or even a graphic, constructed out of characters on the keyboard. While such personalization is encouraged, overlong or controversial signatures can provoke adverse comment. E-mailers can be configured to add a signature to e-mail messages automatically. You may need to create the signature in a separate file first.

Reply

Your e-mailer will have a facility to reply to a received message. Your reply is usually more meaningful if you add your comments underneath the appropriate text of the original message. **Top posting** is simply replying in one section over the sender's original message.

Aliases and address book

To avoid having to type e-mail addresses for regular correspondents over and over again, your e-mailer should allow you to set up **aliases** (also known as nicknames) which link short names (e.g. Jane) with full e-mail addresses (e.g. J.X.Smith@bl.uk). You have only to enter the short name when addressing e-mail. Your alias list functions like an **address book** for e-mail identifiers. If someone e-mails you first, your e-mailer ought to be able to create an alias from the address details in their message.

Attachments

It is possible to send **attachments**, additional non-text files such as images or word processed documents, along with an e-mail. Look in your e-mailer for a command 'Attach Files'. Once you have written your text message you will need to tell the e-mailer where to pick up the file you want to attach: you can do this by browsing through your system and selecting the file. The **multipurpose internet mail extensions** (MIME) standard, which all e-mailers support, encodes attachments as text, and then decodes them back into the original for the recipient.

Return receipt

When you have sent an e-mail to someone, how do you know whether it has been received and read? Your e-mailer ought to allow you to set a **return receipt** which will generate an e-mail confirmation to you when your e-mail has been opened. Even without a receipt you can assume your e-mail is in the addressee's incoming mailbox if the message does not **bounce** (returned to you because of an error, typically an incorrect address). If all else fails all e-mail systems have a **postmaster** which is an address used by the person who oversees the operation of the e-mail system. Trying asking the postmaster if you get no response from a person on their e-mail system.

Overload

The classic problem of using e-mail is **overload**. Initially you will get few messages, mainly from your immediate contacts. Then, as you start to depend on e-mail as a vital communications tool, your mailbox will contain more and more new e-mail each time you look at it. It is impossible to quantify overload. Some individuals despair with more than ten messages to read; others can deal happily with hundreds. There are essentially two ways of dealing with overload:

- Tackle it head on and read e-mail frequently, dealing with it as it comes so you never have old unanswered e-mails when you check for new e-mail.
- The other method of dealing with overload is to never read or reply to e-mail! Ignoring e-mail is not a sensible strategy.

E-mail can span the globe in minutes. It is very cheap, even for those using commercial internet access providers (see Chapter 8). Perhaps the most important advantage of e-mail is the connection with people that it brings.

DISCUSSION LISTS

As well as sending e-mail to individuals, it is also possible to send e-mail to a **discussion list server**. This is a piece of software which stores a list of e-mail addresses of individuals. It can then copy a message from one of those individuals to all the individuals on the list. Thousands of lists have been set up on the internet, each devoted to a particular topic, and intended for people who share a common interest to seek, disseminate and discuss information. In this book we generally use the term **discussion list** which reflects the participative nature of most lists.

Many people use e-mail for communicating with their colleagues. However, many opportunities can be gained by using it to contact people working in a similar job because they face similar problems. Sharing problems is a good way of solving them. Questions that cannot be answered by any reference source can be asked on an appropriate discussion list and can often bring a flood of responses. While this facility does not work fast enough to be of use at a library reference desk, it is nevertheless impressive. E-mail brings experts from all over the world into your reach. And, more than answering the occasional question, membership of a good discussion list brings up-to-the minute news, views and even gossip on a topic that interests you. There is no substitute in other media for this. Serials, even when produced daily, are behind the times. Radio and television have not got the focus or depth an expert needs. No other medium allows the level of interaction with groups of people that e-mail gives.

Joining lists

Joining a list is usually a simple matter which involves sending a standard e-mail message to the address of the discussion list server (listserver@ site-name) leaving the subject line blank. Instructions on joining will be returned by e-mail. When you join a list you will receive a standard welcome message by e-mail, containing further instructions such as how to contribute messages and to unsubscribe. It is advisable to keep this in a folder for future reference so you can see what discussion lists you have joined and can find commands to leave them, etc.

In theory, there is no limit to the number of discussion lists you can join. Some discussion lists are **moderated**, which means that there is a person who vets postings (messages sent to the discussion list) to ensure their appropriateness, and who may admit only individuals who are truly interested in or knowledgeable about the topic. Since being a moderator involves a lot of work, most discussion lists are **unmoderated** and these may carry trivial, erroneous or inflammatory postings as well as messages which do fulfil the purposes of the list.

When you join a discussion list, you will find that postings come with subject lines attached. Replies or further discussion will use the same subject line, usually preceded by 'Re:', indicating a reply. Replies to your postings may take a while to come in. Many messages never generate any replies while others may start intense debates. When you reply to a posting, include some of the text of the original message. It is not necessary to include all of it, but just enough so that someone who did not see the original posting can follow the debate. Not all discussion lists allow subscribers to post messages. Some function solely as sources of announcements.

If you are responding to a posting on a discussion list, ask yourself whether it is really appropriate to reply to all the participants or just to the original sender. Before you dispatch your reply, check whether your e-mailer is sending it to the discussion list or to the person who posted the message. Some personal replies to postings are inadvertently sent to the entire membership of a discussion list.

It is important to distinguish between the e-mail address to which you send subscription requests and the e-mail address of the discussion list itself to which you send your postings. Do not send subscription requests to the discussion list address. When you follow discussion lists, you will see the occasional subscription message incorrectly posted by would-be subscribers.

Following lists

Some discussion lists, if they are particularly busy, offer subscribers a **digest** option which, if chosen, means that you get all the postings made over a time period (typically a day) batched and sent to you in a single e-mail. While this reduces the number of e-mail messages you receive, digest e-mails can be very large and slow to skim through to get to the postings that interest you.

Since incoming e-mail is usually sorted in order of arrival, this mixes up e-mail from different discussion lists with personal e-mail. An e-mail **filter** is a feature of most e-mailers which automatically saves incoming mail to different folders according to rules (instructions) that you define. For example, e-mail from discussion lists can be stored in separate folders, one for each list. This leaves only personal e-mail in your incoming mailbox. If you are short of time, you can just deal with your personal e-mail. The only disadvantage is that you may forget to read and delete e-mail from the other folders.

E-mail from mailing lists can quickly accumulate over holiday periods and at other times when you are unable to read it. One way of dealing with this is to unsubscribe from your chosen mailing lists when taking holiday and then resubscribe when you return. Most mailing lists keep archives of postings (retrievable either by special commands to the mailing list server or viewable via a special web page) so you can skim through messages you missed if you take this option. Another method is to temporarily halt mailing list messages. To do this, you need to send a special **stop** command to the discussion list server addresses of each discussion list to which you subscribe, and similarly a **resume** command to receive messages again. There is another potential problem related to mailing lists and holidays. If your e-mailer has an **autoreply** feature, to be used to inform people who e-mail you that you are away from work, it is wise not to use it if you stay subscribed to discussion lists while away. A message from a mailing list could trigger your autoreply, which goes to the discussion list and is then copied to you as a member of that list, prompting another autoreply, etc. This can create hundreds of 'I am out of the office' messages being sent to every discussion list subscriber very quickly!

If you get into problems remember that a discussion list does not run unattended. A **list owner** is a person who oversees the operation of a particular discussion list. The e-mail address of the list owner is usually included in the subscription details for a discussion list.

Within librarianship and information science, discussion lists focus on particular professional or research specialisms (e.g. government documents, collection development, information retrieval). Others bring together people who work in a particular type of library (e.g. map, music or law), who use a particular type of system or software (e.g. CD-ROM networks or personal bibliographic software) or who belong to the same professional organization (e.g. the Chartered Institute of Library and Information Professionals). Still others have a geographic focus (e.g. library automation in Greece) or are intended for people with a similar job or status (e.g. students, educators).

The Washington Research Library Consortium has compiled a specialist directory of Library-Oriented Lists and Electronic Serials, www.aladin.wrlc.org/gsdl/cgi-bin/library?p=about&c=liblists, and there is a section devoted to UK-focused library lists on the JISCMail Service, www.jiscmail.ac.uk/mailinglists/category/Library.htm. Mailing Lists – Directories, http://directory.google.com/Top/Computers/Internet/E-mail/Mailing_Lists/Directories/, contains listings of discussion lists which span all topics.

NETIQUETTE

Misunderstandings of meaning are possible with e-mail; as a consequence, informal rules of **netiquette** – of how to conduct an e-mail conversation – have evolved.

- When sending e-mail to an individual, try to make the meaning of the text of your message as clear as possible. E-mail is a form of communication which is much less formal than traditional paper mail, but which does not carry any clues as to emotional undertones, as, say, listening to a person's voice in a telephone conversation would.
- Assume nothing about the recipient (in terms of knowledge, emotional state or general background) unless you have met them and know them well.

Netiquette in discussion lists

Netiquette is even more important when posting to a discussion list – you have no idea who may be receiving a message. Some discussion lists have little or no message traffic. Not everyone who is a member of a discussion list posts to the list; members who just read postings sent by other people are known as **lurkers**. There is nothing wrong in being a lurker! Discussion lists, just like any social gathering, are dominated by a few people who do most of the 'talking'. Again there is nothing wrong in this; feel free to join in if you have something to say.

The basic rule for posting to a discussion list is to keep your contribution to the topic of the list. Unmoderated discussion lists, however, are sometimes prone to off-topic messages and also to **flames** – messages which are phrased in a heated and sometimes abusive manner. Unless you enjoy public argument, avoid sending flames and thus getting involved in 'flame wars'.

If an inflammatory or totally off-topic posting is made to a discussion list you follow, wait at least 24 hours before complaining about it. Other subscribers will probably express the same concerns as you. For a flagrant breach of netiquette (for example, an off-topic unsolicited advertisement), you can complain to the list owner of an unmoderated list or, more seriously, to the postmaster at the site where the offending message was posted. If you inadvertently make an off-topic posting to a discussion list, a swift apology should settle things.

THE 'ART' OF TROLLING

Troll is internet jargon for someone whose mission is to upset others. Perhaps the unique feature of the internet as a communications medium is the ease and breadth of opportunity trolls have to practise their 'art', which runs from mild teasing to extremely upsetting racist/sexist abuse. With identity reasonably fluid (through multiple sources of e-mail addresses) and many ways to access the internet, trolls can go unpunished. The Brawl Hall, http://brawl-hall.com/pages/, and the Subtle Art of Trolling, www.urban75.com/Mag/troll.html, are archives of unabashed unpleasantness. They are countered by the Anti-Troll FAQ, www.hyphenologist.co.uk/killfile/anti_troll_faq.htm, and How to Handle a Troll and Beat Them at their Own Game, www.angelfire.com/space/usenet/, which give excellent advice on how to recognize and deal with trolls. The classic academic account is Moral Panic and Alternative Identity Construction in Usenet, www.ascusc.org/jcmc/vol7/issue1/baker.html, which tells the story of a troll's attempt to disrupt discussion about the soap opera Melrose Place. Crank Dot Net, www.crank.net/usenet.html, is the best archive and news service regarding trolling.

Never think that trolls will not affect you. If you use e-mail, read conferences or offer users forums to discuss your services then you will meet one one day. Be prepared.

FAQs

Before posting a question to a discussion list, make sure that the answer is not already available as a **FAQ** (frequently asked question). You can ask for responses to your questions to be sent to you personally. Remember to give your e-mail address. Thank any respondents and distribute a brief summary of your answers via the discussion list. The best way to get questions answered is to get known, for example by having answered other people's questions before. When asking a question, always say how you have tried to find the answer yourself.

As well as the basic rules of netiquette there are many more, which are appropriate in different circumstances.

A good starting point is the Beginner's Guide to Effective E-mail, www.webfoot.com/advice/email.top.html. For more advice, there is a big collection of netiquette guides at Internet – Etiquette, http://directory.google.com/Top/Computers/Internet/Etiquette/?il=1. Perhaps the only significant point to add to their recommendations is to avoid using British colloquialisms or metaphors which may not be understood abroad.

Jargon

To reduce the time spent keying text, there are abbreviations and jargon terms in common usage. **Newbie**, for example, is a person new and inexperienced in internet lore. Many abbreviations can be deduced from their context, e.g. **BTW** for 'by the way', **IMO** for 'in my opinion'.

The Jargon File Resources site, www.catb.org/~esr/jargon/, contains a definitive glossary of abbreviations used in e-mail.

Smileys (also known as emoticons) have evolved to add a measure of emotional undertone to text messages. Created from keyboard characters, they are to be imagined as a face laid sideways, for example:

:-) is a smiling face (indicating humour)
:-(is a sad face (indicating regret).

There are lots of smiley lists at ASCII Art – Smileys, http://directory.google.com/Top/Arts/Visual_Arts/ASCII_Art/Smileys/?il=1. A good place to start exploring netiquette is the Netlingo Homepage, www.netlingo.com/. Finally, never believe everything you see in e-mail: Hoaxbusters, http://hoaxbusters.ciac.org/, is a great site for recognizing hoaxes.

MALICIOUS SOFTWARE

Because of its prominence as the internet application that everyone uses, e-mail is the infection medium used by types of malicious software. They arrive disguised in attachments, apparently sent by a colleague, which, once opened, will release a hidden piece of malicious software as well as whatever content is in the attachment. There are essentially three types of malicious software:

- **Worms** simply spread themselves and cause harm by using up system resources.
- **Viruses**, like worms, spread themselves but also have a **payload**, a harmful function which is triggered by an event (e.g. Friday the 13th triggers random file deletion).
- **Trojans** may offer a useful software function or may conceal themselves. Like viruses they carry a payload but the payload is much more sophisticated than simply a file deletion routine. A password **sniffer** seeks and e-mails outside private passwords; a **network analyser** looks for and leaks security flaws; a **zombie** routine makes a machine perform internet functions on external command.

Counter measures

Some sensible precautions can be employed:

- Outlook, the most commonly used e-mailer because it comes with Windows, is a prime target for malicious software. Using another e-mailer (see above for the E-Mail Software site, which has many e-mailers to choose from) can help to reduce risk.
- Be very wary of opening attachments even from close colleagues. If an attachment is not expected and does not look work-related then query it with the person to whose e-mail it is attached. Clever viruses use **social engineering** (techniques to appear a normal part of operations): a virus might take two individual e-mail addresses for Individuals A and B from the e-mailer on an infected machine owned by Individual Z and send an infected attached to B so that it appears to come from A, thus concealing Z as the owner of the infected machine.

You may get spurious e-mail warnings that viruses can be spread by just reading a certain e-mail. This is nonsense.

All types of malicious software can be detected by **anti-virus scanners**, software that has a database of program code snippets which identify each known worm, virus and trojan. Scanners are effective, but new worms, viruses, etc. appear all the time; their database of identification code snippets needs to be constantly updated. It is good practice to have a virus scanner on each and every machine you have and to keep its database as current as possible.

While organizational networks are normally rigorously defended, there is often a window of vulnerability for viruses to exploit. One machine without an up-to-date virus scanner can be compromised and as such become a

Internet Hoaxes, E-Mail Rumors, Urban Legends, http://urbanlegends.about.com/ library/blhoax.htm, is an excellent resource debunking internet myths.

Anti-Virus, http://directory.google.com/Top/ Computers/Software/Shareware/ Windows/Security/Anti-Virus/, is a collection of links to anti-virus scanners with free trial versions.

threat to other machines on its networks by its virus scanner software. In January 2004 the MyDoom worm caused chaos worldwide, using both e-mail and file sharing networks such as Kazaa to infect vulnerable systems. In 2001 the Code Red worm wreaked havoc on the internet, even infecting Microsoft's own systems, and more recently the SQL Slammer worm took just ten minutes to replicate itself across the internet, impacting on systems as diverse as airline reservations and ATMs at banks. The ability of such viruses to cripple large organizations is something that should be of great concern to information professionals in terms of their own productivity and service delivery.

Spam and phishing

Revealing your e-mail address on your organization's website, in a posting to a mailing list or conference (see Chapter 6) or by submitting it to suspect websites can get your address on a **spam list**. These are enormous collections of e-mail addresses which are bought by unscrupulous individuals who use them to send out unwanted advertisements, known as spam. Some people **munge** (deliberately obfuscate their e-mail address, e.g. John.Smith@removethistoemailme.somelibrary.org.uk) to keep them spam-free but this is a hopeless undertaking. Many organizations are now using **spam filters** to automatically detect and remove spam in incoming e-mail. Some e-mailers incorporate them.

However, spam filters are not foolproof and care should be taken in trusting excessively in their efficiency.

> Spam Filters, http://directory.google.com/Top/ Computers/Software/Internet/ Clients/Mail/Windows/Tools/ Spam_Filtering/?il=1, is a useful collection.

A recent development in spam e-mail is **phishing**, which is the use of spam lists to send out fake official e-mails to those lists. These fake e-mails will purport to come from your bank or another company, and will require you to go to

Never reply to any spam e-mails you receive, and never purchase anything from a spam advertisement! An advertiser who sends out millions of spam e-mails for next to nothing only needs a few sales from those spam e-mails to make a profit.

a website to enter confirmation details, claim a prize or do another made-up task. The website will be fraudulent and will harvest the details you submit and use them to defraud you! It is very difficult to recognize phishing e-mails from genuine official e-mails. It can be done by checking the veracity of the website they refer you to (see Chapter 8 for how to check ownership of websites). The best policy, sadly, is to delete each and every 'official' e-mail you receive, unless you are expecting that e-mail because of a recent purchase, etc.

The cleverness of phishing scams will continue to evolve: the Anti-Phishing Working Group, www.antiphishing.org/, is a good place to keep up with the latest phishing tricks. Protect Yourself from Internet Scams, www.scambusters.org/, takes a wider view of internet scamming.

SECURE E-MAIL

E-mail seems very private. You send an e-mail to an individual, so only two people know what is in that e-mail. E-mail also appears easy to delete. These are completely false assumptions.

E-mails can be read when they transit the **e-mail servers** that organizations maintain to run their e-mail service. They can also be read (albeit with more difficulty) as they are routed from the sender to the recipient via a chain of computers on the internet. E-mails will be stored while in transit on e-mail servers and intermediate machines. Governments, concerned about maintaining law and order, are increasingly requiring that e-mails be stored. Organizations, worried by legal liability of the contents of e-mails, are also storing them. So deleting your copy of an e-mail may remove only one of many copies of that e-mail.

There are other potential problems. The recipient of your e-mail message could forward it to someone you had not intended. It is never wise to send sensitive information by e-mail! It is difficult, but not impossible, to fake the identities of the senders/receivers of e-mails. E-mail content can also be altered in between the sender sending it and the recipient getting it.

The basic rule is not to use professional e-mail accounts for private or social purposes. Personal web mail accounts (see above) should be used for private/social e-mail. Always send each and every work-related e-mail in the expectation that anyone anywhere will be able to read it – unlikely as this is! Backup all your incoming and outgoing work e-mails on a regular basis and only then delete them from your e-mail folders. This is a sensible precaution if the content/date of sending/receipt of an e-mail ever becomes a bone of contention.

Encryption

If you are worried about privacy or security (e.g. sending sensitive information by e-mail) then use **encryption**. Encryption software works by encrypting (scrambling the content so as to hide words) your text into a near-random string of characters, using a **pass phrase**. This pass phrase is required to get the encryption software to change the encrypted message back into text. Some e-mailers offer basic encryption facilities.

There are two problems with using built-in e-mailer encryption:

- The recipient must be using the same e-mailer.
- Even more crucially, you must somehow send the password to the recipient. Sending the password in an ordinary e-mail defeats the purpose of using encryption in the first place, since that password can be intercepted.

Public/private key encryption gets around this problem. Encryption is linked to two machine-readable keys: a **public key**, which can be sent by ordinary e-mail and a **private key**, which is kept on your own computer. To communicate, both parties exchange public keys by ordinary e-mail. The sender then encrypts a text message using their private key and the public key of the recipient. This encrypted message is then sent to the recipient by e-mail. To decrypt this message the recipient needs their private key and the public key of the sender. This process not only removes the need for sending a password but also means that, using keys, each party can verify that the other party was the sender/recipient and that the content of the message has not been altered in transit. A freeware program, Pretty Good Privacy (PGP) has become the de facto internet standard for this means of communication.

PGP can be downloaded from the International PGP Home Page, www.pgpi.org/.

There are problems with public/private key encryption.

- You need to trust that an individual's public key really does belong to that person.
- Public/private key encryption is viewed askance by some government security agencies because it can defeat their attempts to decrypt messages. This has led to restrictions on its use though there are no current restrictions on its use in the UK.
- Merely using encryption signals that you have something you want to hide!

The Cryptography site, http://world.std.com/~franl/crypto.html, explores these issues in great detail.

As well as hiding the content of a message, there may also be a need to hide the identity of the sender. Anonymous e-mail is rightly frowned on in some quarters, but it has legitimate uses. For example, it is vital to the Samaritans who can now be contacted by e-mail and need to preserve the anonymity of their callers. Anonymous e-mail is achieved using a **remailer** – a computer at an intermediate site which accepts an e-mail with a normal identifier which it strips off before forwarding the e-mail to its intended destination.

See Anonymous Mailers, http://directory.google.com/Top/Computers/Internet/E-mail/ Anonymous_Mailers?tc=1/, for sites which offer this facility.

INTRODUCTION

USENET is a global **conferencing system**. A conferencing system is similar in purpose to a discussion list, in that each conference (or **newsgroup** in USENET terminology) is based on one topic. It differs in that readers of a newsgroup read a common pool of messages which make up that newsgroup, rather than receiving individual copies of each message in their own mailbox.

USENET CONFERENCING

There are currently around 100,000 newsgroups. Newsgroups are organized into **categories**, the most important of which are:

Category	Topic
bionet	biology
biz	business
comp	anything to do with computers
rec	games, sports and hobbies
misc	topics that don't fit anywhere else
sci	the physical sciences

soc	the culture of countries or social groups
talk	debates on controversial topics
news	topics on USENET itself
alt	'alternative' topics.

The precise topic of a newsgroup is indicated by a hierarchical name, which starts with a category, for example:

Newsgroup	Topic
comp.mail.eudora	the Eudora e-mailer
rec.arts.books	novels
sci.maths	mathematics
soc.culture.iran	Iran.

TILE NET, www.tile.net/news, provides a complete listing of all USENET newsgroups, including a short description of each one.

Like discussion lists, some newsgroups are moderated, which means that postings are screened before appearing. Most newsgroups are not moderated. This can lead to extremely bizarre and/or offensive postings (especially in the 'alt' newsgroups).

Each newsgroup contains one or more **articles** (messages). Articles in USENET newsgroups look very much like e-mail postings. Like e-mail messages, they have the name of the person posting them and a subject. Each article has a unique identifying number. Some articles are replies to earlier articles. An article and its replies are collectively known as a **thread**. Articles in the same thread have the same subject header.

Newsreaders

To access USENET you need a **newsreader** client. Just as with e-mailers, there are different clients, available either as separate programs or included with other applications, like web browsers or e-mailers. Which you use is a matter of availability and personal preference.

Download.com's Newsreaders, www.download.com/Newsreaders/ 3150-2164_4-0.html?tag=dir, is a collection of newsreader clients.

All newsreaders operate on three levels:

- The first level is to display a list of subscribed-to newsgroups, i.e. newsgroups you have chosen to read, together with the number of articles (and possibly threads) they contain. Your newsreader will allow you to move between newsgroups and choose one to read. It will also allow you to see newsgroups that you have not subscribed to and to subscribe to any of them. You will also be able to unsubscribe from (i.e. leave) newsgroups.
- Selecting a newsgroup moves you to the second level of newsreader operation which is to show the articles/threads in the newsgroup. A newsreader will show only threads and the number of articles they contain. Each thread has a subject and the name of the person who submitted the first article.
- The last level of newsreader operation is the display of articles/threads themselves. If you select a thread, you will then see the first article of the thread. You will be able to read the rest of that article (if it does not fit on the screen) or move on to the next article in the thread.

When you have finished reading articles which interest you in a particular newsgroup, you must use your newsreader to **mark as read** all articles in that newsgroup. This records for that newsgroup the current highest article number, so that when you open it later, only articles posted with higher numbers will be shown. Your newsreader records read article numbers in a file (usually called **newsrc**). This lists the newsgroups you have subscribed to and the number of the last article you have read in each of those newsgroups.

If this all seems very cumbersome, it is actually easier to read USENET than discussion lists. In your mailbox, messages from different discussion lists are intermixed. Replies to one of your messages may be interspersed throughout your mailbox with messages on other subjects. In contrast, each newsgroup is self-contained. A threaded newsreader can compress many articles into threads and show you on one screen the total activity of a newsgroup.

Following newsgroups

For the newcomer though, USENET can be daunting. With e-mail you start with an empty mailbox. With USENET you can start automatically subscribed to hundreds of newsgroups. Follow some simple rules:

- Unsubscribe to all groups, except for a few that really interest you.
- Only read threads that look interesting to you.
- You do not have to read every article in every thread.
- Get to recognize who posts articles you find most relevant.
- Read the initial articles in the longest threads (these are obviously of interest to the newsgroup audience).
- Remember to mark all articles as read before you leave the newsgroup, so that next time you will see only new articles.
- Use a facility offered by most newsreaders called the **kill file**. A kill file is a stoplist of subject words or individuals' names which, if attached to an article, prevent that article from appearing in your newsreader. This

facility shields you from idiots and uninteresting topics.

- If you find a particularly relevant article in one newsgroup, look to see if it has been **crossposted** (posted to more than one newsgroup simultaneously). These other newsgroups might also be of interest to you.

MSR Netscan, http://netscan.research.microsoft.com/Static/, is a free tool that creates detailed reports on the activity of a chosen newsgroup. It is useful in deciding whether to follow that newsgroup.

Where does the pool of messages that form USENET come from? Your newsreader will enable you to post a message to a particular newsgroup. This message is then relayed to neighbouring sites which take their **newsfeed** from your site. These sites will pass on your message and eventually it will reach every site which takes USENET. Incoming messages reach your site in a similar manner, being passed along a chain of newsfeed sites. USENET resembles the decentralized mode of operation of P2P file sharing because there is no central mode.

Before you post to a newsgroup, be sure you have read the FAQ document, if one is published for that newsgroup. This document is a compendium of the newsgroup's wisdom and is guaranteed to answer obvious questions that might be asked about the topic of the newsgroup. FAQs are normally posted on a regular basis to a newsgroup, at least once a month. For the seeker after information, a FAQ can be invaluable. There is a USENET newsgroup which publishes nothing but FAQs, called news.answers.

The Internet FAQ Archives, www.faqs.org/faqs/, provide a repository of all USENET FAQs.

It is imperative to follow netiquette when posting to newsgroups, just as when posting to discussion lists.

Accessing USENET

Not all sites take USENET and those that do may not take all newsgroups. There are several reasons for this. The volume of articles added daily to USENET is immense and requires a lot of central disk storage at a site. As a result articles are expired after a set period (which varies between sites) and deleted to save storage space.

> If you miss articles on your local newserver, Google Groups, http://groupsbeta.google.com, offers a searchable archive of all mainstream newsgroups.

Perhaps the main reason why not all newsgroups are taken by many sites is concern over their content. Many newsgroups in the 'alt' category are conduits of all sorts of strange and sometimes unpleasant postings. The newsgroups in the alt.sex hierarchy have been widely shunned because of worries over their explicit pornographic content. Some of the newsgroups in the alt.binaries hierarchy are sources of illegal copyrighted files. Lots of alt newsgroups have no sensible purpose: alt.flame, for example, exists only to provoke heated argument. But, just as it is unfair to judge a newsagent only by its top shelf, USENET contains many stimulating, erudite newsgroups. The advantages of USENET then are very similar to those of e-mail discussion lists. If the name of a newsgroup does not sound inviting, and a glance at its contents reveals nothing of interest, then move on and look elsewhere.

You may not be able to access USENET because your internet service may not support a newsfeed. In this case there are two options:

• Access Google Groups via your web browser and use it to read news.
• Point your newsreader at a public-access news server.

> Newzbot, www.newzbot.com/, gives a list of public-access news servers.

Whatever your personal choice of newsgroups, there are currently only two library/information oriented newsgroups, soc.libraries.talk, http://groups.google.co.uk/group/soc.libraries.talk?hl=en, and comp.internet.library, http://groups.google.co.uk/group/comp.internet.library?hl=en.

WEB-BASED FORUMS

USENET, although well-used, has never been a mainstream attraction of the internet since many people simply do not know it exists. Newsreader clients have never been on as many desktops as e-mailers and web browsers. Google Groups, because it is web browser accessible, has helped to open up USENET. However, conferencing itself is very popular.

A conference is so much more convenient than a mailing list, especially if it is accessible via a web browser. There is much software that runs on web servers that provides conferences (also known as **forums**, **message boards** or **bulletin boards**).

A definitive listing of conference software can be found at Forum Software, http://thinkofit.com/webconf/forumsoft.htm.

Organizations use forum software to let their employees and/or customers connect. Individuals can add a forum to their website so their users of that website can interact with each other.

Message Boards – By Topic, http://directory.google.com/Top/Computers/Internet/On_the_Web/Message_Boards/By_Topic/, is a browsable hierarchy of forums by subject area, while Message Boards, http://directory.google.com/Top/Computers/Internet/On_the_Web/Message_Boards/, links to forums supporting ranges of topics. Library and Information Science – Chats and Forums, http://directory.google.com/Top/Reference/Libraries/Library_and_Information_Science/Chats_and_Forums/, is a listing of library-related forums. BoardReader, www.boardreader.com, provides a word search facility for web forums and is useful in finding web forums that might be of interest to you.

If no forums appear of interest then it is easy to start one of your own on a topic you want.

Hosted Components and Services – Message Boards, http://directory.google.com/Top/Computers/Internet/Web_Design_and_Development/Hosted_Compone nts_and_Services/Message_Boards/, lists an enormous range of hosting services for forums, some of which are free. Yahoo! Groups, http://uk.groups.yahoo.com, is a popular host (its forums work through both web and e-mail), as is Google Groups which at the time of writing was launching a forum creation facility alongside its USENET archive.

Blogs

A specialized form of web forum is a **blog**, a contraction of the term **web log**, which is a personal record kept in public view on the web. These are currently very popular.

Lists of blogs can be found at Library and Information Science – Weblogs, http://directory.google.com/Top/Reference/Libraries/Library_and_Information_Science/Weblogs/, and Weblogs, http://directory.google.com/Top/Computers/Internet/On_the_Web/Weblogs/.

Perhaps this is the end result of the democratization of publishing that the internet has engendered, in that we are all publishers now and should all be running our personal blogs!

Daypop, www.daypop.com, and Feedster, www.feedster.com, are both search engines which focus on blogs.

Many blogs include RSS feeds (see Chapter 1) from other sites or blogs and offer their content as RSS feeds.

BLOGGING, PODCASTING AND 'CAMCASTS'?

One of the first blogs to make headlines outside the internet was Where is Raed, http://dear_raed.blogspot.com/, which gave an Iraqi's account of the conflict there. Blogs started to get coverage in the mainstream press, as their commentary-style of content was ideal fodder for quoting to effect. Blogs were heralded as affecting the US election. Criticizing his employer resulted in a blogger working in Glasgow's Waterstones bookshop being sacked. The Blog Site, www.theblogsite.com/, is a handy compendium of all things of interest in blogs and covers these stories and more.

How important are blogs? To their authors they might seem the perfect mode of expression. Reading blogs is an excellent way of picking up views that simply are so unique that they would never get exposure in any other way. However, blogs have a scaling problem. Readers have only a finite amount of time and, as more blogs appear, they must drop old blogs to follow new ones.

Podcasting is the latest variant on blogging: it removes the necessity to write, because podcasts are essentially recorded speech. IPodder.org, www.ipodder.org/, is a useful guide to the sources on offer and the technologies involved. Podcasts can be considered as personal radio stations. The logical conclusion of all this appears to be personal television channels – the ultimate in 'reality TV'? Television Programs – Reality-Based, http://directory.google.com/Top/Arts/Television/Programs/Reality-Based?tc=1/, gives a listing of commercial offerings. Perhaps soon individuals will star in their own 'camcasts', relaying their lives live via personal web cam. A mobile web cam connection is not far off, given the progress towards all-pervasive wireless internet access.

real-time systems

INTRODUCTION

Real-time services involve interaction between two or more users in real time, in other words they are **synchronous** as opposed to **asynchronous** services. The main example of this in the modern use of the internet is real-time chat services, where users carry out virtual conversations with each other using a variety of software solutions. Real-time chat services are often seen as one of the recreational aspects of internet services, and certainly their popularity in this context is undeniable. However, real-time chat also has potential organizational benefits and, from an information and library professional's perspective, can enhance service provision greatly.

INTERNET RELAY CHAT (IRC)

For many years following its inception in 1988, **internet relay chat** (IRC) was the most popular method of chatting online. Special client software is needed to access IRC. IRC allows you to join a **channel** – a discussion. Channels can be public or private (open to only a few people). Individuals on IRC channels tend to be known by adopted nicknames. Using IRC you can list channels, and join and leave channels. Once you have joined a channel, anything you type is echoed to the screens of the other users on that channel, following your nickname. You can list the current individuals on a channel and message them individually if you want.

Conversations on IRC tend to be gossipy. Some sites consider IRC to be nothing but a time-waster and do not allow its use. Occasionally, IRC can have real importance when news events are reported live by eye witnesses via IRC news channels.

INSTANT MESSAGING (IM)

More recently chatting on the internet has been conducted using **instant messaging** programs (IM). IM programs are normally stand-alone programs that are specific to one network: for instance the most popular IM services are MSN, Yahoo! and AOL. Each of these services has its own IM client that needs to be installed on a user's computer to gain access to the chatting network. Like IRC a user must select a username and password to access the network. Once a username has been allocated to a user it remains their online identity and cannot be used by anyone else, unless it is revealed to others or lost. One of the most attractive aspects of IM software is the fact that you can create a list of your friends with whom you chat online, sometimes referred to as buddies' lists, which can then notify you if and when a buddy is online. This makes using such services very spontaneous: a conversation can be conducted without appointment or notice merely by sending your buddy a message when you see that they have logged on.

IM clients have become more sophisticated, and they all now have some value added aspects to them, including the ability to view the web cam of the person who is chatting to you, as well as hear their voice. They also offer the ability to exchange files with other users of the chat service, anything from a picture to a copyrighted file. Many users have their preferred IM client running all the time they are online, making them an integral part of the online experience.

This familiarity with the IM clients that many users have is both a positive and a negative when it comes to providing internet services in libraries. On the one hand, the familiarity means training in the technology is not as big a challenge as it may be for other software; on the other hand, the familiarity may also lead to an expectation that the IM service will be available in a library setting, something that for various reasons a library may not supply.

ACCESS TO CHAT

As will be seen below, the use of IM clients can have enormous benefits for library services, but the fact remains that chatting on the internet, especially chat room access for children and teenagers, creates a political and moral dilemma for library and information professionals.

It is relatively safe to hypothesize that as the internet continues to be a developing medium, and one that mainstream society is just beginning to get to grips with, it is viewed with a mixture of fear and wonder. Whether or not the fear is misplaced is open to debate, but what is certain is that the press in the United Kingdom, especially the tabloid press, are obsessed with the internet and its ability to place children in danger. In March 2001, posing as a 12-year-old girl, a television presenter and internet columnist for the *Sunday People* tabloid uncovered 'a vile web of danger waiting to snare our children' (Vorderman, 2001, 18). The article makes uncomfortable reading as it recounts her experiences in internet chat rooms, being approached by paedophiles attempting to 'groom' children. Whether we agree with the way such stories are presented or not, the fact remains that most parents will have their understanding of chat services delineated by reporting such as this. Even more worrying from the point of view of a library and information professional is the fact that, in the same article, Vorderman recounts an episode where:

121

[a] girl of 15 vanished after chatting to a man of 20 through a computer in her local library. Detectives used mobile phone records to find that she had travelled 170 miles from her Carlisle home to meet the stranger in Hull. She returned home after two days away. (Vorderman, 2001, 19)

There are numerous other examples of such reporting with regards the internet generally and chat rooms specifically that must be taken heed of. As facilitators of access to the internet for many youngsters it is paramount that library and information professionals are aware of such feelings in the general public and are also aware of the real dangers providing such access could bring. Many library services get round the problem by banning access to chat rooms, or restricting access to rooms that are child only. While this gets round the ethical problems of providing access, there are opposite ethical viewpoints that state that providing such access gives a social inclusion function for people who have no access elsewhere. There is no overall solution that all library services can use, but all should try to educate users to the dangers of such services as part of a wider internet literacy programme.

For an enhanced discussion of all the ethical issues in providing such access see *Public Internet Access in Libraries and Information Services* by Sturges (2002).

VIDEOCONFERENCING

As mentioned previously, commercial chat clients such as Yahoo! Messenger or MSN Messenger allow users to view the person they are chatting to by using web cameras. This is a straightforward and inexpensive way of providing videoconferencing; all that is necessary in addition to the computer and the chat client is a web camera, a relatively inexpensive purchase. Issues relating to privacy have to be taken into consideration if used in a library context. For instance, a hypothetical scenario may be a member of the public using a library-based PC with web cam to interact with a government employee in discussing issues of a personal nature. The increasing emphasis on electronic government may see libraries providing such service options in the future, and an area set aside that ensures privacy may be something that has to be considered.

However, there are other solutions available if providing videoconferencing is something that a library service wishes to do in a more formal and higher quality capacity. Software solutions such as Microsoft NetMeeting and CUseeMe are widely used in the commercial sector, and offer a more sophisticated user experience than the free chat clients such as Yahoo! Messenger. Other options include purchasing standalone equipment to provide videoconferencing, normally consisting of a large monitor with a camera either built in or attached to the top of the monitor. These hardware solutions can be expensive but, as their main purpose is to provide videoconferencing, they offer high-quality solutions for the purpose.

THE COMING TELEPHONE REVOLUTION: INTERNET TELEPHONY

For many years the incumbent telecommunications operators (like British Telecom) enjoyed a virtual monopoly on telephone services. That monopoly was recently broken by the advent of mobile telephone services. A third wave of change is in the offing. This wave is being led by internet telephony. The standard use of internet telephony is to connect a caller's computer with a recipient's computer and use a package like Skype, www.skype.com/, to manage the conversation. SkypeOut is a variant on the basic Skype product which allows calls from a computer to a standard telephone or mobile. The quality is not good but it is cheaper as the internet is used to route as much of the call traffic as possible. Even more revolutionary are **VOIP** (voice over IP) phones (see Chapter 8) which route calls through broadband networks, getting both good quality and cheaper calls. They plug into your broadband connection at home. VOIP.co.uk, www.voip.org.uk/, is the best guide to this fast developing area in the UK.

REFERENCES

Sturges, P. (2002) *Public Internet Access in Libraries and Information Services*, London, Facet Publishing.

Vorderman, C. (2001) Your Child is Just Three Clicks Away from an Evil Paedophile, *Sunday People*, (18 March), 18–19.

networking technologies

INTRODUCTION: HISTORY OF THE INTERNET

The internet is made up of thousands of small national and regional networks, which link together to form a global network of computers that can communicate and exchange information. The internet's origins lie in **ARPANET**, commissioned in 1969 by the US Defense Department to provide a secure communications channel for US military research which would be resilient to nuclear attack. ARPANET proved so successful that in 1983 the military use was split off and the remaining service opened up to other researchers. At that point, ARPANET connected 60 universities in the USA, one in Norway and two in the UK. By the following year, over 1000 host computers were connected.

The base network in the UK was **JANET** (the Joint Academic Network, www.janet.ac.uk). Its origins lie in several small scientific networks which were developed in the UK from the late 1960s onwards: for example, the National Physical Laboratory's network established in 1968. JANET was inaugurated on 1 April 1984. In 1991, JANET was directly linked to the internet. JANET is now funded by the **Joint Information Systems Committee** (JISC), www.jisc.ac.uk, of the Higher Education Funding Councils and managed by the UK Education and Research Networking

Association (UKERNA). Now many private networks in the UK have been connected to the internet.

BASIC NETWORKING TECHNOLOGIES
Networks

The two basic types of network are **local area networks** (LANs) and **wide area networks** (WANs). A LAN links computers that are physically close to each other and usually 'hard wired' together via cables. Typically, LANs are used in single organizations at single sites. WANs, however, can cover large distances, within and beyond national boundaries; they are generally connected through telecommunications links, which may use a mixture of advanced technologies such as fibre-optic cables and satellites. It is the wide area networks that are of most concern here.

Computers handle digital data in the form of discrete bits and bytes. Networks typically transmit data in one of two forms, either **analog** (a continuous signal) or **digital**. Most networks, like the internet, use dedicated digital telecommunications lines. Organizations which make heavy use of an external network may install leased telecommunications lines to provide permanent, digital links from their in-house multi-user machines or LANs to external network services.

Protocols

Networks require a common framework of routines and rules to allow computers to communicate with each other. These are called **protocols**. Protocols are technically complex but, put simply, they specify, for example:

- how data are to be encoded for transmission
- the physical transmission media that are allowable

- the conventions for addressing items of data so that they can be delivered to the correct network destination
- the applications (the types of tasks) that are to be supported on the network.

The internet uses the TCP/IP protocol, (Transmission Control Protocol/Internet Protocol). Local networks typically use the **Ethernet** protocol. The main task of a protocol is break down data to be transmitted into **packets** (small chunks with an identifier, a destination and a sender) so that those packets can be **routed** (directed across intermediate connections) and travel from the sending machine to the destination machine.

Servers

Any use of a network involves at least two computers: the one the user is on, and another one that is being accessed for some purpose via the network. The user's computer may be a personal computer directly connected to the network, or a **gateway server** to which the user connects from their own machine which acts as a terminal. The internet generally operates on a **client/server** model. One computer, the client, on behalf of the user, requests services of another computer, the server. At any one time a single server computer can be dealing with any number of client computers. Thus server computers tend to be more powerful than client computers, whose job very often entails merely the display of data passed along from a server.

Bandwidth

The speed and power of the server, and the **bandwidth** (how much data can be moved per second) of the network connection, determine how quickly these services are fulfilled. Dedicated network lines, especially if they are made of **optical fibre**, can handle far more data than an ordinary telephone line can, even using the latest, fastest modems. The limit on data transfer, the bandwidth of a telecommunications line, can still be reached even on the fastest of lines when lots of users try to move vast amounts of data.

Digital networks

There is a trend away from the use of single-function telecommunications lines moving data in analog form (the traditional telecommunications infrastructure) to one in which lines handle data in digital form and can transmit voice, computer data, video, etc. in a single common format. Apart from all traffic using one line, digital lines are easier to upgrade to higher capacity than analog ones. BT recently announced that its core network is to be based on TCP/IP, to exploit this flexibility. This trend is beginning to affect even the standard telephone service. VOIP (voice over IP) offers a voice service over an IP-based network. This service is expected to slowly replace the existing analog domestic and business phone system. VOIP phones plus ionto a broadband connection and function exactly as a 'normal' phone, but rental costs and call charges are lower. They are available now from a range of suppliers, including British Telecom (www.btbroadbandvoice.com) and Sipgate (www.sipgate.co.uk/).

Services – VOIP, http://directory.google.com/Top/Business/Telecommunications/Services/VoIP/, lists services and/or software which use VOIP.

CONNECTING TO THE INTERNET

Your organization may already provide you with internet access (as at academic sites, for example). Alternatively you can pay a commercial **internet service provider** (or ISP), some of which offer low-cost connections aimed at individual users, while others specialize in linking corporate networks, with a range of options (and costs) in between.

Essentially an individual user needs a telephone socket connected to a

> For a listing of ISPs in the UK and the connection services and plans they offer see ISP Review, www.ispreview.co.uk/.

computer with a **modem** (a device which enables computer signals to traverse a telephone line). The modem, under the control of **communications software**, calls a number which, once a user identification and a password have been given, opens a connection into the internet. Just about any sort of computer sold by a computer dealer for business or home office use can be used to access the internet. This is known as **dial-up** access.

Dial-up connections function only while the line is live and modems have reached a ceiling in terms of speed. Increasingly users are opting for permanently 'on' **broadband** connections to the internet, providing the home user with the same level of access as someone working for an organization. These could be provided either by an **asymmetric digital subscriber line** (ADSL), which works over ordinary telephone lines, or **cable modems**, which work on the optical fibre networks of local cable companies. In ADSL data flow faster towards the user (**downstream**), than from the user to the network. This is a good thing since most internet usage is pulling content off the network. Most broadband services are **contended**, shared between a certain number of users. At the time of writing a range of faster speed (greater than 512k per second downstream) broadband connections is appearing. Some are based on a **symmetric digital subscriber line** (SDSL) in which data flow upstream and downstream at the same rate.

> Broadband Help, www.broadband-help.com/home.asp, is an authoritative guide to broadband services and suppliers.

Not all locations in the UK can access broadband: some are too remote from a telephone exchange that offers ADSL. **Integrated services digital network** (ISDN) connections will be available and these are always on, but their speed is not much faster than modem dial-up. **Satellite broadband** is currently the only option for broadband in these locations: satellite broadband, however, suffers from **signal lag** in between the ground and the routing satellite in orbit. This significantly hampers highly interactive services (see Chapter 7).

Home networking

Home networking is growing because of always-on broadband domestic connections. This involves sharing the single broadband connection among a number of computers (e.g. the parental work laptop and the children's recreational desktop). Such sharing requires a **router**, a device hitherto seen only in workplace networks, and means of connecting devices. Wires can be used but more convenient (and less unsightly in the home) is **wi-fi** (wireless-fidelity) which is an implementation of the networking Ethernet protocol which works without wires. A wi-fi capable router broadcasts and receives data and each connected device needs a wi-fi network **card** (add-on which gives a new facility). Increasingly, devices such as **internet radio receivers** and **digital music players** are being linked into home networks. The day of the networked fridge is not far away!

DIY Home Networking Guides and Tutorials, www.homenethelp.com/, is good for information on this fast developing area.

Internet on the move

Mobile internet connections have appeared: they do not require a wired connection and operate in public places. Wi-fi connection points (known as hotspots) have been offered in busy public places (e.g. train stations, hotels, airports, etc.), some provided by wi-fi service providers and some by chains of shops (e.g. Starbucks). For a subscription a laptop or a PDA with a wi-fi card can be connected within range of a wi-fi server. **Roaming** enables a customer of one wi-fi ISP to use the connection points of another. However, wi-fi connections are short range (around 50 metres) and not yet ubiquitous.

> Intel's Hotspot Finder, http://intel.jiwire.com/, is the best global guide to hotspots and has links to wi-fi service providers. FreeNetworks.org, www.freenetworks.org, lists free wi-fi hotspots throughout the world, provided by people willing to share their broadband connections.

Mobile phone companies are offering internet connections wherever a mobile phone signal exists. Many mobile phones come with **general packet radio service** (GPRS) which is always on and transmits digital data at around the same speed as a modem. A new generation, **3G** (3rd generation), is also always on but connects at near broadband speeds. These connections are meant to deliver internet facilities (like e-mail and web) to a mobile phone but small screen size and tiny keyboards make mobile phones (and related devices like the Blackberry) fiddly to use. It is possible to connect some mobile phones via wires or wirelessly, using the limited range networking protocol **Bluetooth,** to laptops or PDAs, which have bigger screens and better keyboards. Mobile internet connections are, at the time of writing, expensive because they are charged on data transmitted, but it is expected that charges will fall, as they have in the fixed-line internet connection market. Of course, if you lack the appropriate technology (mobile phone and/or laptop) then your choice of internet connection on the move will be restricted to **cybercafés.**

> For a searchable list of cybercafés see Cybercafes.com, www.cybercafe.com/.

USING THE INTERNET ON THE MOVE

Mobile internet services are currently very much like fixed line dial-up services were ten years ago, i.e. slow, unreliable and expensive. GPRS connections are not ubiquitous. Areas outside cities or major transport links have few GPRS connections. 3G is being rolled out only in big cities. 3G connections promise high speed but do not seem to deliver. Content provider plans to sell streamed music and video over such links might well be premature. Some services provide automatic connection detection (between GPRS, 3G and wi-fi), leaving the user to choose the fastest (or cheapest) available. Charging by content sent and received is fair but very disruptive of internet use patterns. (Why bother to turn off graphics in web pages or eschew downloading e-mail in case someone has sent a large attachment?) uk.telecom.mobile, http://groups.google.co.uk/group/uk.telecom.mobile?hl.en, and 3G Forum, www.3g.co.uk, are good sources of advice and opinions.

SITE ADDRESSING – HOST AND DOMAIN NAMES

People and resources on a network have to have a **site** that is defined in terms of an address of a computer on the network. Thus people are located by the particular computer they use, and information resources by the computer on which they are stored. On the internet, computer names are made up of two parts, a **host name** and a **domain name**. A domain name is similar to the STD or area code in a telephone number. It tells you where the computer is, and what organization owns it. A host name is an identifying name for a computer within a domain, just like a telephone number identifies an individual in a particular area. Here are some typical examples:

- www.bbc.co.uk
- www.ukoln.ac.uk
- www.homeoffice.gov.uk.

132

Domain names are normally in three parts and read right to left. The right-hand part identifies the country of the domain. Most countries have a two-letter country code – uk for the United Kingdom, de for Germany, etc. If there is no country code, then the United States is implied although there is a 'us' code which is occasionally seen. To the left of the country code is a code showing organization type. In the UK domain these are:

ac	academic
co	private company
gov	government
org	non profit-making organizations.

A number of new domain names were introduced in 2001/2. They include .biz, .info, .name and .pro as well as .aero, .coop and .museum.

In domains for other countries, organization type codes may vary. For example, domains in the United States and Australia use 'edu' for an academic organization, while in most European countries 'ac' is used. To understand the organization type in a domain name, a little judgement is called for.

The last element in a domain name is an abbreviated name for an organization. Thus Leeds Metropolitan University is abbreviated to 'lmu' and the University of Bath to 'bath'. Some organizations are recognizable; others are not. The host name is the final element. It can be something mundane (like 'hp3' for the third Hewlett Packard minicomputer) or it can be something more memorable (like 'sloth').

There are exceptions to these conventions such as:

- portico.bl.uk
- pipex.net.

In both the above, there is no organization type code.

Host and domain names together identify a computer on the internet. An alternative form of computer name that can be used is the **IP address**. This is a string of four numbers separated by full stops, e.g. 138.38.32.45 for UKOLN. These numbers are used in the actual addressing done on the internet and an automatic translation is made (invisibly to the user) of host and domain names into numbers, by a system known as the **Domain Name Scheme** (DNS). The DNS scheme is managed by a non-profit organization called **ICANN**.

Domain names can be valuable commodities. A company is usually very concerned to get a domain name that either matches its company name or is appropriate for its service/product. ICANN oversees a number of

accredited domain-name **registrars** around the world who are responsible for assigning and maintaining domain names.

> Nominet, www.nominet.org.uk/, is the ultimate registrar for .uk domains.

The internet may be difficult to use and understand primarily because the resources it contains have no physical presence for a user, other than on a computer screen. Host and domain names not only locate people and resources but can also help the user to infer something more about new resources as they are discovered. Thus a UK television schedule provided by www.bbc.co.uk (the BBC) ought to have more authority than one provided on sloth.cs.du.edu, a computer (host name 'sloth') located at the Department of Computer Studies at Denver University in the United States (a hypothetical example). This is only a guiding principle, not a universal rule.

Domain names are commercial properties. **Domain squatting** is the strategy of buying domain names expected to be wanted by big companies or rich individuals later, to whom they can be resold at profit. **Typo squatting** is the practice of buying domains identical in name to very popular domains (e.g. www.gogle.com) except for a minor typo. Mistakes which cause people to arrive at these domains still bring in substantial traffic. Typo squatting can be used in conjunction with phishing (see Chapter 5) to create almost convincing fakes of other domains (e.g. www.nationalwestminsterbankuk.co.uk instead of www.natwest.co.uk, the real one!).

WHOIS

How do you know who owns a domain? **WHOIS** is an internet search facility of the ICANN domain registries. It can be searched either via a client search package or a website which offers this facility, such as Arin WHOIS Database Search, www.arin.net/whois/. **IPBlock** is a related search function which turns an IP address into a domain name.

Traceroute

Domains can also be used in diagnosing internet-related problems. An internet connection fault (e.g. a website does not load) can either be the fault of your internet service provider in which case you can contact it with the problem, or it might be a fault somewhere else on the internet. The most useful facility for diagnosing where internet problems lie is **traceroute**. It can be used via either a client search package or a website which offers this facility. Traceroute shows you each machine or router on the internet that traffic from your machine to another machine (e.g. a website) traverses. Using this display you can see where the problem occurs – in your ISP, at an intermediate stage or at the final site you are trying to access. The traceroute display shows graphically where a break occurs.

For a global listing of browser-based traceroute tools, which can route to a destination site and also back to your own address (so that together the paths show how packets flow between your machine and the website you are trying to reach) see Traceroute.org, www.traceroute.org/. The London Internet Exchange, the main switching point for internet traffic into/out of the UK, provides a public traceroute facility at Network Tools, www.linx.net/www_public/our_network/network_tools/. A client package that performs all the above functions is Sam Spade, www.samspade.org/ssw/.

SECURE INTERNET

Your internet connection can be spied on at the packet level by **packet sniffers** (software which records packets and their contents) anywhere between your machine and the packet's destination. Packets reveal your machine's IP address and from this someone can find out who owns that machine, where that machine is located and who provides its internet connection. Looking into the contents of packets will reveal what services you are using, and possibly critical details like your passwords, your credit card number, etc. If the IP address of your machine is discovered then **port scanner** software on a hostile machine can probe your machine's internet connection looking for a way into your machine to plant trojans (see Chapter 5). **War driving** is cruising using special software to detect private unsecured wi-fi connections and illegally using them for internet access.

What can be done about these security weaknesses? The internet was never designed with security in mind so solutions are not easy to use nor all-encompassing.

Wireless LAN Security, www.wardrive.net/, gives advice on how to lock-down wi-fi networks.

Port scanners can be defeated by a **firewall** which watches and blocks unauthorized external accesses to a machine (and watches outgoing connections). Firewalls can be software-based or hardware-based (most routers have one).

Zone Alarm is an example of a firewall for Windows systems. It has a freeware version downloadable from Zonelabs, www.zonelabs.com/. A firewall must be configured to stop or allow certain outgoing or incoming connections although they do have default settings.

Passwords and credit card details can be hidden by encryption (scrambling characters). This can be done by **secure sockets layer** (SSL) which is used by internet shops: its activation is shown by the padlock symbol in the lower bar of your browser. **IP spoofing** software can hide your IP address as can public or for-pay anonymizer websites.

WebTunnel from Primedius, http://www.primedius.com/, is client software which hides your real internet address, while Proxying and Filtering – Hosted Proxy Services, http://directory.google.com/Top/Computers/Internet/Proxying_and_Filtering/Hosted_Proxy_Services/ ?il=1, is a directory of online anonymizer services.

Finally **virtual private network** (VPN) software can encrypt all your packets, if they are being sent to a chosen destination that can host its own matching VPN software, e.g. you are working at home and connecting up to your office remotely.

Virtual Private Networks, http://directory.google.com/Top/Computers/Security/Virtual_Private_Networks?tc=1/, lists VPN facilities.

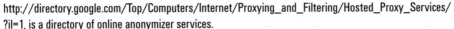

9 libraries and the internet

INTRODUCTION

The impact of the internet and the world wide web on society has been profound. For the information and library profession this impact has been exacerbated because of the nature of what the internet and web exist to do. At the root of both the medium and the profession is the provision of information, and there can be little doubt that the web has fundamentally changed the role of information provision to the public. In this vein providing internet access is seen by many as a natural extension of the library's remit to provide information, education and leisure services to users. The internet and web open up enormous possibilities for the development and delivery of library and information services. They offer an intuitive and increasingly familiar computing environment through which to deliver existing services, and a progressive channel for developing new ones. Services can be offered beyond the physical constraints of the library building to a wider and more diverse customer-base.

This chapter discusses some of the issues relating to the impact of the internet and the web on specific library sectors and services.

ACADEMIC LIBRARIES

Academic librarians in the UK have been working in a richly networked environment for many years, with access to the internet being freely available at point-of-use through the nationally funded **joint academic network (JANET)** service. It is therefore not surprising that academic libraries were among the first wave of institutions to pioneer the development of internet services and web pages. Today virtually all UK higher education and many further education libraries offer publicly available web services. National libraries and a number of national research and information centres, also linked to JANET, were similarly quick to establish web presences.

While the first academic library web pages offered little more than factual information about the library itself and links to external sites, it was not long before the web was exploited as a gateway to library resources and services. Conversion of the OPAC to web access was often the initial starting point but this was quickly extended to making available other electronic collections – both existing and newly digitized. Academic and research libraries are still at the forefront of research and development into how best to develop and deliver electronic information resources. Information delivery is happening increasingly, though by no means exclusively, via the user's web browser.

Follett Report, 1993

In 1993 the Follett Report looked in detail at higher education in the UK; it emphasized clearly a vision and enhanced role for library services (Joint Funding Councils' Libraries Review Group, 1993). The major effect of this on academic libraries was to emphasize the role of ICTs in delivering services for an ever-expanding student base. While the core of the subsequent spending on libraries came in the form of refurbishment of libraries and their infrastructures, a major component of Follett was the creation of the **Electronic Libraries Programme** (eLib), www.ukoln.ac.uk/services/elib/, which aimed to research into some potential solutions for delivering ICT-based library services. With funding through the programme, which ran from 1995 to 2001, researchers investigated a whole range of topics from the digitization of text and image collections to document delivery and on-demand publishing of books and journal articles as and when needed by students and academics. The projects funded under the eLib programme varied, but at the core was an emphasis on moving towards the hybrid library. The hybrid library concept emphasized the need to move gradually from traditional paper-based library services towards digital library services where appropriate.

Another result of research into digital libraries in the UK was the development of **subject gateways** such as EEVL, HUMBUL, OMNI (now called BIOME) and SOSIG. Gateways provide searchable and browsable catalogues of selected internet-based resources. Some of these gateway projects were brought together to form the **Resource Discovery Network** (RDN), www.rdn.ac.uk/, in 1999 and the service now provides eight subject-based gateways covering all of the major academic disciplines.

In addition to those resources developed by the academic community almost all academic libraries have subscriptions to commercial electronic databases such as Ingenta, Proquest or Emerald. To the student or academic using such services the links found from the library web page should make access seamless. Authentication issues have been largely addressed as a result of the **ATHENS** system, www.athens.ac.uk/: one password per user, which can last them for the duration of their studies, is all that is necessary for access to a multitude of resources.

The internet and web lie at the heart of these service improvements, and there is little doubt that the library services of academic institutions in the UK in 2005 vary greatly from those of 1995.

PUBLIC LIBRARIES

UK public libraries, hampered by lack of government support, huge
demands on their budgets and lack of time for research and development,
were understandably slow to follow the lead of their academic colleagues.
There were isolated exceptions, such as the pioneering work undertaken
on **CLIP** (Croydon Libraries Internet Project). A main theme of this project
was to examine the potential of the internet as a reference tool (Batt,
1995). Issues concerning provision of and public response to network
services generally were also explored in the CLIP project, and in others
such as Solihull's **IT Point.**

Generally, however, public library response to the internet was slow to
get off the ground. According to a national survey of internet connectivity
in UK public libraries conducted in 1995, although 53% of public library
authorities had some sort of internet connection, most of them were
restricted to use by staff only – generally one or two workstations to
support reference services (Ormes and Dempsey, 1995). Nationally there
were only 39 public access workstations available. In 1994, **Project EARL**
(Electronic Access to Resources in and through Libraries) was initiated as
a coalition of interested parties within the library and information
community to co-ordinate the development of electronic networks for
information, and to facilitate the exchange of information and experience.
EARL's approach was pragmatic, offering help and advice to member
authorities.

In a groundbreaking report entitled *New Library: the people's network*,
the Library and Information Commission examined how public libraries
could and should exploit information and networking technologies (Library
and Information Commission, 1997a). This report and its sister publication,
Building the New Library Network (Library and Information Commission,
1997b), led to a transformation in the ICT infrastructure for public

libraries and the internet

libraries across the UK. The documents laid out a vision for all public libraries in the UK to provide high-quality access to the internet for their customers by provision of funding to purchase the ICT equipment and bandwidth. The resources were provided by the **New Opportunities Fund** (NOF), a national lottery-sponsored agency. The money was allocated to each local authority on the basis of its population and number of service points; the effect of the policy on the services provided in public libraries, notwithstanding the physical infrastructure of the buildings and skills of the staff, has been immense.

While many librarians in public libraries had been used to providing an element of internet service to their customers before the expenditure was rolled out in 2002/3, the programme also catered for a wide-ranging training programme for library staff. The basic level is the **European Computer Driving Licence** (ECDL), www.ecdl.com/main/index.php; more advanced training involves skills such as advanced web searching and web design. The emphasis then was on imparting the skills to staff to enable them to help customers utilize the new resources and create bespoke information gateways for their users using web technologies. As well as the creation of the infrastructure for the public to access the internet a heavy emphasis was also placed on content creation to ensure the public had access to high-quality resources when they went online. The **NOF-Digitise programme**, www.mla.gov.uk/action/pn/nof-digitise.asp, funded digitization projects, with the emphasis on creation of local resources. The resulting resources created, accessible via the portal Enrich UK, www.enrichuk.net/, show a great diversity in content and focus, and represent material from all corners of the UK and for all interests. This socially inclusive and educational emphasis is ongoing and reveals the very real concern that the public requires to have resources created for them that are relevant to their lives. Librarians stand at the forefront of this content creation, and the skills necessary involve a thorough understanding of the internet and web technologies.

A focus for public libraries in the future will be electronic government, or **e-government** as it is more commonly referred to. As community focal points, public libraries are ideally placed to reach socially excluded members of society, and with a widespread concern at the levels of civic engagement with the democratic process both local, devolved and central governments are making great use of the web to reach the public. In the UK the emphasis is on ensuring all government services that can be will be made e-ready by the end of 2005. For many government departments this may involve merely providing a web-based resource for the downloading of forms, while for others it will involve actual engagement with users in consultation exercises, providing the ability to file tax returns and the like.

The portal Directgov, www.direct.gov.uk/, provides access to e-government sites from all strands of British government.

SPECIAL LIBRARIES, NATIONAL LIBRARIES AND INFORMATION UNITS

Only a small proportion of UK private sector libraries offer a public access website. More typically, the UK corporate librarian is involved in the design, development and maintenance of web pages for in-house consumption on the corporate **intranet** (internal internet/web service) rather than providing a public service. Many web initiatives which began in libraries of all types have become the responsibility of the parent organization, with dedicated staff and a committee structure, editorial board or steering group to advise on the design, content and structure of the website and on the management of the project. The library itself will often make a strong contribution to this development team and, depending on local policy, will have more or less autonomy for the look, feel and content of its own pages on the organizational site.

National libraries alone have been able to implement and develop their websites according to their own criteria. As such, they offer a rich mix of facilities, ranging from OPAC access and readership information to a portal for their nation's culture online.

> The European Library, www.theeuropeanlibrary.org/portal/index.htm, is a portal to Europe's national libraries while **IFLA** (International Federation of Library Associations) maintains a global listing of national libraries, www.ifla.org/VI/2/p2/national-libraries.htm.

DIGITAL LIBRARIES

The term digital library started to appear in the literature in about 1993, although there is a bewildering variety of definitions for digital libraries, depending on the discipline in which the term is used, because research into digital libraries often calls on a mix of disciplines including LIS, computer science, sociology, politics and psychology.

The Digital Library Federation, www.diglib.org/, came up with the following definition:

> Digital libraries are organizations that provide the resources, including the specialized staff, to select, structure, offer intellectual access to, interpret, distribute, preserve the integrity of, and ensure the persistence over time of collections of digital works so that they are readily and economically available for use a by a defined community or set of communities.

Notable examples of digital libraries are:

- **Project Gutenberg**, http://gutenberg.hwg.org, uses volunteers to digitize out-of-copyright material in the humanities. It dates from 1971 and is possibly the oldest digital library in existence.
- **The Association of Computing Machinery (ACM) Digital Library**, http://portal.acm.org/dl.cfm, gives access to the contents of ACM journals, magazines and conference proceedings.
- **THOMAS**, http://thomas.loc.gov, is run by the Library of Congress and is a comprehensive collection of federal legislation.
- **Networked Digital Library of Theses and Dissertations (NDLTD)**, www.ndltd.org, is maintained by a federation of universities around the world.

These examples show that digital libraries vary by content sources and types, sponsoring organization(s) and user services. This diversity will only increase over time.

THE CHANGING ROLE OF THE LIBRARY AND INFORMATION PROFESSIONAL

Technological change has affected libraries, but what of librarians? At its core the role of the librarian and information professional has not changed in the digital age. What has changed is the mechanism for delivering the information to the customer. There is a strong argument for suggesting that librarians are vital in the skills chain in terms of imparting knowledge of the internet to the customer, regardless of sector. Crucial also is the continuing importance of **information literacy** skills, greatly lacking in many members of the public who see the web as the panacea for their information seeking. The explosion in cases of **plagiarism** in higher education due to the readily available wealth of materials in electronic form is one example of where this is proving a challenge. Development of robust and up-to-date information literacy programmes is a vital part of the training regime of any library and information service. The legal framework has changed to accommodate new technological developments. Copyright is now a thornier issue, because of the ease of copying and transfer of digital content.

Filtering and blocking

Filtering is a software-driven process whereby access to certain materials is blocked before it is loaded by the web browser and raises new ethical issues. The user is normally presented with an image on the screen telling them this, with some software solutions even defining for the user the reasons why the material is blocked. In **keyword blocking**, filtering software simply looks for offensive words in the URL of the website, or in the content of the web pages before they load up. This is perhaps the most controversial way of filtering content, because it does not take into account the context of the words being blocked, meaning that perfectly innocent sites may be blocked. In **site blocking**, sites stored centrally are blocked. This can be a more sophisticated way of filtering inappropriate content, as at some point a human being has consciously chosen to block a site. Blocks can be removed.

As well as understanding how to utilize web technologies on behalf of customers the growing emphasis for the future will be **content creation** using web technologies. As has been stated, 'many commentators see the future of the library profession in assuring information quality rather than in direct end-user support or in the acquisition of information sources' (Brophy et al., 1998, 30). There remains a pressing need for library and information professionals to become experts in the internet and web technologies not in any way to replace their core skill set, but to allow them to bring their vital skills into the organization of the wired world.

REFERENCES

Batt, C. (1995) *The Library of the Future: public libraries and the internet*, paper presented at the 61st IFLA General Conference, 20–5 August, 1995, www.ifla.org/IV/ifla61/61-batc.htm.

Brophy, P., Craven, J. and Fisher, S. (1998) *The Development of UK Academic Library Services in the Context of Lifelong Learning*. Manchester, CERLIM, www.ukoln.ac.uk/services/elib/papers/tavistock/ukals/ukals.html.

Joint Funding Councils' Libraries Review Group (1993) *Report*, HEFCE (on behalf of the Councils), Bristol, www.ukoln.ac.uk/services/papers/follett/report/.

Library and Information Commission (1997a) *New Library: the people's network*, London, Library and Information Commission, www.ukoln.ac.uk/services/lic/newlibrary/.

Library and Information Commission (1997b) *Building the New Library Network*, London, Library and Information Commission, www.mla.gov.uk/information/legacy/lic_pubs/policyreports/building/.

Ormes, S. and Dempsey, L. (1995) *Public Library Internet Survey – First Report*, London, Library and Information Commission, www.ukoln.ac.uk/publib/lic.html.

internet applications in libraries

INTRODUCTION

This chapter explores the impact of the internet on libraries by examining internet-related changes in vital service categories. The internet makes 'virtual reference' possible, as well as increases the need for users to have deeper information literacy skills while they are surfing alone in lieu of professional guidance. Cataloguing has had to change from its traditional focus on books to the variety of digital resources found on the world wide web or in institutional digital repositories. Metadata is slowly taking centre stage as a result. Materials now increasingly either appear in digital form or acquire digital form through digitization. The move away from physical materials has led to proposals for open access to academic journals and to the creation of special collections of digitized resources. Finally, access to this richer and vaster mix of materials needs much more careful guidance, via subject portals (which collect and organize hand-picked resources in particular disciplines) and via personalizable institutional portals, which try to mediate between the complexities of the internet-based information landscape and the needs of the user for quick, easy access to relevant information.

ONLINE REFERENCE SERVICES

Reference services in libraries, especially academic libraries, have been transformed by internet technologies. As well as providing the resources that answer some of the questions asked by users, internet technologies provide novel ways of delivering reference services. **Virtual reference** has been coined as the term for these emerging services. Patterson defines this as, 'any reference activity conducted through an electronic medium' (Patterson, 2001, 209). The basic concept is that patrons with a query can literally be anywhere and use the internet to ask a librarian a question and receive the answer. Obviously the key aspect to virtual reference services is access and response time or, as Moyo states, 'availability of the service to the user at the point of need, and a minimal turnaround time for patrons to get the answers and/or help they need' (Moyo, 2004, 224).

Some services run on the basis that there will always be a librarian available online for a set time each day, while others work on the basis of an e-mail or form-based query received that is then passed on and answered. An example of the latter model can be found in the numerous **Ask a Librarian** projects that exist. In the UK a public libraries consortium developed the following model:

Ask a Librarian (www.ask-a-librarian.org.uk/) is an example of a web-form service in which questions can only be initiated from a designated Website. The library on duty for that day receives all enquiries submitted, regardless of subject, as e-mails. How library staff choose to handle the questions varies from library to library. While there are some smaller libraries where only one librarian handles the questions, quite a few libraries divide the questions up among branches, departments, or subject specialists. If they have a difficult question, they can circulate it to their Ask colleagues via a closed [internet] discussion list.   (Berube, 2004, 33)

This is an excellent example where the technologies, rather than replacing the skills of the reference librarian, reinforce the importance of the skills librarians have. Using a network of reference librarians to answer the queries received in turn, users always have a skilled gatekeeper on hand to answer a query. As Chowdhury has discussed, 'it is doubtful whether digital libraries can totally replace human experts and personalised services' (2002, 278). Services like Ask a Librarian reinforce this on a daily basis and, rather than the librarian and the internet being an anathema to each other, they prove an inspiring double-act for the patron.

While Ask a Librarian in the UK uses an asynchronous model, other virtual reference services opt for a synchronous model using internet chat technologies. Most notably the Library of Congress offers virtual reference services to support its American Memory digitization programme, a librarian being available for two hours each afternoon to answer virtual queries from patrons (Library of Congress, 2005). Curtis and Greene discuss a similar service at the University of Nevada, where the service responds to not merely traditional reference queries but also questions about University issues that might ordinarily be considered administration problems (2004, 220). This is something, they believe, that expands their 'concept of "information" and our role in helping people find it' (2004, 232). It has to be said that such an approach also gives the library a greatly enhanced profile within the institution and provides an excellent use of human resources. What better way of putting the library at the centre of the University than by providing out-of-hours guidance to students on University life. Developing this theme, it has been argued that virtual reference services actually enhance the role of the librarian in terms of becoming a partner with a student in their learning. As Ellis has stated:

> In these new digital environments, users and librarians have discovered new
> relational dynamics. The digital reference engagement has transformed users from
> being anxious, dependent, and disinterested in learning, to being self efficacious,
> autonomous, and proactive learners.   (Ellis, 2004, 116)

Virtual reference services are just one example of how internet technologies have transformed the role of the librarian in a proactive way.

INFORMATION LITERACY

LIS professionals have long recognized the need to help users develop good information skills and this has become all the more crucial now that these users are turning increasingly to the internet to support their information seeking. There are many initiatives to embed general **information literacy** skills in the UK education sector. The key skills in the National Curriculum include the use of ICT and information handling within schools and, following a review by the Qualifications and Curriculum Authority (QCA), www.qca.org.uk/, in 2000, these key skills were recommended for post-16 learners and later extended to 14–19 year olds (QCA, 2004). While information literacy skills are not explicitly referred to in the key skills curriculum they are implicit within the ICT aspect of the qualification.

The Society of College, National and University Libraries (SCONUL), www.sconul.ac.uk/, developed the 'Seven Pillars of Information Literacy' (SCONUL, 1999); this was intended to provide a practical working model to help develop information literacy skills training and curriculum design within higher education. See Figure 10.1 (overleaf).

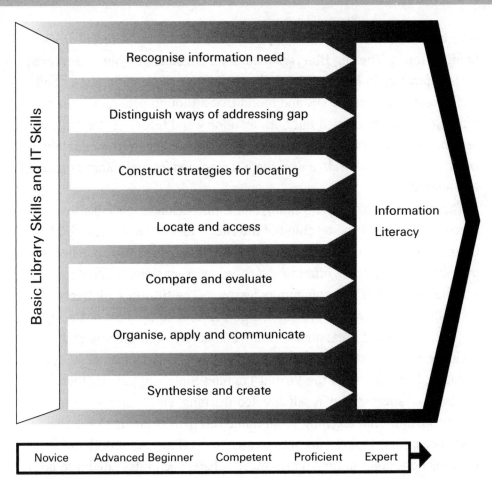

Figure 10.1 SCONUL Seven Pillars Model for Information Literacy
© Society of College, National and University Libraries (reproduced with permission)

This model recognizes that basic library skills and IT skills, although distinct proficiencies, are both necessary building blocks to becoming 'information literate'.

The planning and delivery of information skills training differs according to sectors and institutions but it is traditionally an area in which LIS staff have had a major role and this appears to be increasing. A recent JISC-funded project, The Big Blue, www.library.mmu.ac.uk/bigblue/, surveyed current practice in information skills training for students in higher and further education in the UK and found that although generally information training was being carried out both by library and teaching staff this was very rarely done as a joint venture. One of the project's recommendations was that more collaborative work between academics and information staff was needed.

There are several online training and skills packages available to specifically support the teaching of internet information skills. One of these is the RDN Virtual Training Suite, www.vts.rdn.ac.uk/, a collection of over 60 online tutorials offering self-paced internet skills training for academic and adult and community learning. The tutorials are freely accessible and, as well as providing a guided tour to the best of the web for a particular subject area, offer training and advice on searching and critically evaluating information found via the web. An informal survey conducted on the use of the Virtual Training Suite suggests that while it can be used successfully in self-directed learning, embedding such training into an institutional teaching programme can help students to see the relevance of developing internet research skills (Place, 2005). Below are some real examples of how these tutorials have been integrated into both academic teaching and library skills training:

I am a Learning and Teaching Co-ordinator with responsibility for promoting the effective use of technology in teaching and learning. I work with individual academics to encourage them to use technology in their teaching. There is considerable variety in experience amongst staff across the university and I find that RDN often provides the solution to their problems. The Virtual Training Suite (VTS) gives people a valuable introduction to using the Internet and finding materials for teaching. It appeals to academics, as the materials are relevant to their discipline. Indeed, I have seen senior staff bouncing up and down in enthusiasm as they find good things for the first time! One of the most important parts of VTS is that it introduces the idea that internet resources need to be evaluated and how to site web references a skill that many of our staff lacks. At the other end of the spectrum, many academics already use learning technologies effectively in their teaching are introducing their students to RDN.　　(Learning and Teaching Co-ordinator, HE)

We've been using this since it was first launched, as part of our induction to key skills. This gives them a few of the evidence requirements for building an evidence portfolio at level 1. We find they are often already familiar with the 'shopping basket' technique and engages the student through[out] this process. It stimulates healthy discussion throughout the session.

It also satisfies one of the new requirements of the 2004 key skills standards by asking the student to 'Present evidence of purposeful use of e-mail'. Once the student has completed the tour and has collected all the useful links, we ask them to e-mail a copy to the tutor and themselves as evidence.

(Key Skills/Basic Skills Co-ordinator, FE)

At the Fire Service College we recommend the RDN VTS on a number of our internet training sessions (ranging from courses for firefighters to senior officers in the UK fire service) and have various of your leaflets in the library that anyone can pick up. We do not know what take up there is and do not assess.

(Library Manager, Fire Service College Library & Information Resource Centre)

I teach at Palmer College of Chiropractic in Davenport, Iowa, USA. I use the tutorial for Allied Health Professionals in my course 'Principles of Chiropractic and Health Sciences Information Literacy,' which is a required course in the second trimester of our Doctor of Chiropractic program. This is the students' very first assignment, basically to refresh them with the research process and familiarize them somewhat with health science resources. I have worked up my own hardcopy worksheet based on the tutorial, which they turn in to me the week after I assign the tutorial. So far it is the best tutorial I have found dealing with the health sciences.

(Information Literacy/Reference Librarian)

The provision of ICT training and support has also become a major activity for public libraries following funding from the **People's Network** to introduce community access to the internet (MLA, 2004). Libraries have tackled this in a variety of ways, from formal instruction to the creation of value-added services to help users find and use information. One example of this training is provided through a partnership between Denbigh and Conway Library Services, who are offering free open learning training in basic ICT skills to the public. Complete beginners are given two introductory sessions to get them started, but otherwise users can work through the course at their own pace with support from booklets and tutor guidance if needed.

In a slightly different approach The Real Project, www.intoreal.com/, in Glasgow is working with a number of learning organizations to offer support and access to a range of learning resources, from bite-sized learning resources to fully accredited courses.

CATALOGUING INTERNET RESOURCES

It is important that librarians get involved in cataloguing and organizing internet resources because they have the core skills required not only to catalogue but also to evaluate and select those resources. Traditionally libraries created bibliographic records only for materials that they physically held in their collections. However, users' demands for access to internet resources and other electronic materials have required libraries to step outside this traditional role and begin to provide this access. There are two main approaches to cataloguing internet resources:

- using traditional cataloguing practices such as **MARC** and **AACR2** to create bibliographic records of internet resources to fit into a library OPAC. OCLC was an early experimenter of this method with the introduction of the **CORC Project**, which used the traditional co-operative cataloguing model to create MARC catalogue records for internet resources. Although CORC is no longer running, all the features developed during this project were incorporated into the new OCLC Connexion Service, www.oclc.org/connexion/, in 2002.
- cataloguing internet resources using **metadata**. Metadata are structured data about data that are used to describe internet resources. **Subject gateways** are a good example of this approach, involving the expertise of librarians to select and describe internet resources using metadata. They are covered in detail below.

There are pros and cons to both approaches. Library-cataloguing formats such as MARC are complex processes developed to describe print materials, which tend to be static in nature. Unlike printed materials, internet resources are far from static; they grow and change on a regular basis or sometimes disappear altogether without warning. Metadata formats such as the **Dublin Core** have been developed specifically to describe electronic sources of information and, as such are more lightweight and flexible to these changes. The Dublin Core, http://dublincore.org/documents/dces/, is a set of 15 elements (or fields) that has been developed by the library and networking community to provide an international standard for describing internet resources:

- **Title** – the name of the work
- **Creator** – the person(s) primarily responsible for the intellectual content of the work
- **Subject** – the topic addressed by the work
- **Description** – outlines the content of the work
- **Publisher** – the agent or agency responsible for making the work available
- **Contributor** – the person(s), such as editors and transcribers, who have made other significant intellectual contributions to the work
- **Date** – the date of publication of the work
- **Type** – the genre of the work, such as novel, poem or dictionary
- **Format** – the physical manifestation of the work, such as Postscript file or Windows executable file
- **Identifier** – string or number used to uniquely identify the work
- **Source** – other works, either print or electronic, from which this work is derived, if applicable
- **Language** – language of the intellectual content of the work
- **Relation** – relationship to other works
- **Coverage** – the spatial locations and temporal durations characteristic of the work
- **Rights** – a statement of the intellectual property rights applicable to the work.

As the name suggests the Dublin Core is an attempt to define the most basic set of elements needed to describe a web resource. In reality many of these elements are enriched by the use of **qualifiers** to refine a particular element, for example the subject element might be extended by a qualifier that describes the use of a particular classification scheme, e.g. Dewey Decimal Classification (DDC) or Library of Congress Subject Headings (LCSH) to describe the topic of the resource.

As well as Dublin Core there are other specialist metadata schemes that have been created to deal with the particular needs of a subject or domain:

- The **data documentation initiative** (DDI), www.icpsr.umich.edu/DDI/, is a standard for describing social science datasets in data archives.
- The **encoded archival description** (EAD), www.loc.gov/ead/, is a standard for describing archival finding aids such as inventories, registers and indexes that are created by the archives, libraries and museum sector.
- The Institute of Electrical and Electronics Engineers (IEEE) has developed a standard specifically for describing educational learning and teaching materials. This has recently been adapted for use in a UK educational context, and is called the **UK LOM Core**, www.cetis.ac.uk/profiles/uklomcore.

These specialist schemes are valuable for their particular communities but are generally quite complicated and expensive to create and maintain. Choosing a format from the variety of existing metadata schemes will depend upon various factors, including availability of time, staff, and the needs of your users.

> The IFLA site Cataloging and Indexing of Electronic Resources, www.ifla.org/II/catalog.htm, has a good overview section on cataloguing and indexing electronic resources.

DIGITIZED COLLECTIONS

Digitization of special collections such as incunabula, rare photographs, maps, sound archives and other materials can help to solve the dual problems of preservation of and access to rare or fragile materials.

American Memory from Library of Congress, http://memory.loc.gov/ammem/, has done much pioneering work.

E-journals

E-journals can be defined very broadly as electronic serial publications and can include traditional academic publications, newsletters, magazines as well as **zines** (small publications usually produced by an individual and not-for-profit).

The advent of electronic journals has revived some of the early traditions of academic publishing, whereby readers would enter into a correspondence with the original author. This is easy to do electronically, and in this sense the electronic journal blurs the distinction between a publication and a discussion forum and can potentially turn an article into a living document.

Most of the traditional academic journals now offer electronic copies alongside the print version (and in some cases offer only an electronic version). In the UK JISC has been involved in setting up a national scheme for the licensing of academic electronic journals on behalf of the further and higher education community.

The National Electronic Site Licensing Initiative (NESLi2), www.nesli2.ac.uk/, provides a model licence, which is used in annual negotiations for over 9000 scholarly journals and 11 major publishers in the UK and abroad.

E-prints

There is currently a great deal of interest in the academic community in the 'self-archiving' of research, due in no small part to shrinking library budgets and increasing costs from publishers . An **e-print** is an 'electronic publication', usually an electronic copy of a research article. These can be either pre-prints, i.e. copies of articles submitted to a journal for peer review, or the final drafts of articles (these may or may not be peer reviewed). An **e-print archive** is a central database or repository of articles and/or metadata describing the content of articles.

> These may be organized by subject such as CogPrints, http://cogprints.ecs.soton.ac.uk/, at the University of Southampton or RePEc, (Research Papers in Economics), http://repec.org/. Increasingly more common are institutional archives, often run by library or information services staff at universities. Some early examples of institutional archives in the UK are at the University of Glasgow, http://eprints.lib.gla.ac.uk, and Nottingham University, http://eprints.nottingham.ac.uk/.

The House of Commons Science and Technology Committee's recent inquiry into scientific publications resulted in a report *Scientific Publications: free for all?*, www.publications.parliament.uk/pa/cm200304/cmselect/cmsctech/399/399.pdf, which recommended that all UK higher education institutions should establish institutional repositories for their published output and that research councils and the government should take responsibility for implementing a co-ordinated approach. However, although the report was welcomed by the Government, it looks unlikely that it will be willing to adopt the role of co-ordinating such an approach.

Open access publishing

Interest in e-prints and **open access publishing** (access is free to academic users) is shown by funders such as the Wellcome Trust who have issued a statement in support of the establishment of free-access, high-quality journals available over the internet. Some publishers are also beginning to embrace open access journals.

> The Public Library of Science (PLoS), www.plos.org/, is trialling a method of charging the author of the article a fee for disseminating their work and BioMed Central, www.biomedcentral.com/, has an agreement with the JISC to allow UK researchers to publish and access their peer-reviewed journals for free.

Many e-print archives make use of the Open Archives Initiative (OAI), www.openarchives.org/, which is an interoperability framework and standard for the development of e-print archives. The OAI-PMH (OAI-Protocol for Metadata Harvesting), www.openarchives.org/OAI/openarchivesprotocol.html, provides a simple method of making the metadata from archives available for harvesting, allowing information from a number of archives to be aggregated together into a single database. An example of such a service is OAIster, www.oaister.org/o/oaister/, at the University of Michigan which brings together details of articles from around 400 institutions.

PORTALS

The concept of a portal can be quite confusing because the term can be used to describe a variety of different services depending on the sector in which it is used. A very general definition of a **portal** is the presentation of a variety of facilities and information sources through a single interface, typically through the web. The original idea of portals is that they provide 'one-stop shops' for users. However, in reality it is unlikely that a single portal can be all things for all people and users still have to choose which portals suit their needs.

Library portals

Most current information discovery services provide only fairly shallow linking to information on the internet, that is to say they guide users in the direction of useful sites and sources but it is then often left to the user to navigate within these sources to find the exact piece of information they require. Library portals take this one step further by bringing together library catalogues with a range of online subscription databases, selected free internet content, e-journals and learning and teaching materials. Typically users can search across these different types of information concurrently and the search results are presented as a single list. Some examples of commercial library portal products include MetaLib, ZPORTAL and Encompass. In order for these services to work effectively **single** sign-on (SSO) authentication needs to be in place, i.e. users are required to authenticate themselves only at the start of a session in order to get access to all the resources and databases they are allowed to use. Many library portals also offer **OpenURL** services so that users can be guided from the page of results to the most appropriate copy of a resource.

For more information on OpenURL see the OpenURL for Framework Context-Sensitive Services, www.niso.org/committees/committee_ax.html.

Institutional portals

There is currently a great deal of interest in creating institutional portals, especially in the UK academic community. Similar to library portals they provide a variety of online resources to support learning, teaching and research but in addition they offer access to local administrative and management services such as finance, registration, etc. A recent investigation into institutional portals in higher education found that some of the key motivations for developing these portals were streamlining information and services; improving services to students and staff; offering personalized services and improving administration efficiency (Englert, 2003). In terms of functionality they have considerable overlap with **content management systems** (CMS, see Chapter 3) and **virtual learning environments** (VLE) and in many cases may actually incorporate these within the institutional portal (see Figure 10.2).

Institutional portals are sometimes referred to as **thin portals** because they gather together relevant content and services but users are actually accessing a number of different services underneath, whereas **thick portals** provide more fully integrated access. There are a number of commercial and open source software solutions for building institutional portals, including UPortal, Oracle Portal and Jetspeed.

163

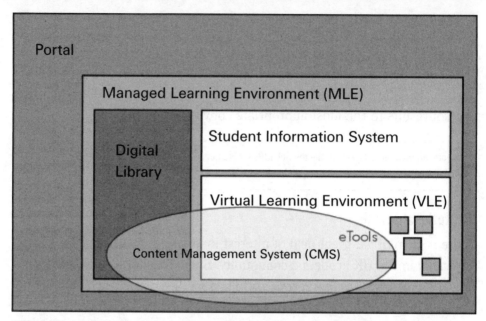

Figure 10.2 Possible components of an institutional portal (Browning, 2002)
Reproduced with permission.

Personalization

Despite portals, users are becoming increasingly overwhelmed by the amount of information available to them on the internet and many websites now offer some degree of **personalization** to try to alleviate this problem. Personalization can be defined as 'the ability of a Network Service to be shaped or re-shaped so as to better meet the individual needs or wants of a user' (Ferguson and Schmoller, 2004). The most common personalizable aspects allow users to choose content and how it is displayed within a service. Portal sites typically offer personalizable services.

INTEGRATED INFORMATION SYSTEMS

VLEs

Virtual learning environments (VLEs) are integrated online systems designed to provide interaction between learners and tutors and to support flexible and distance learning. They provide authorized access to course modules or curricula, which can be customized for individual courses and/or users. Typically VLEs include student registration information, course details, access to learning materials and communication support including e-mail, bulletin boards and chat facilities. In addition they also provide a number of administrative facilities for tutors such as being able to track an individual's length of time on the system, what content has been accessed, etc.

> A number of commercial VLEs are available: Blackboard, www.blackboard.com/, and WebCT, www.webct.com/, are used widely.

However, because they are proprietary systems they can be somewhat inflexible in adding functionality that is not provided out of the box and some institutions have chosen to create their own learning environments.

MLEs

Managed learning environment (MLE) is a term used to encompass the whole range of information systems and processes of a college or university, from learning and teaching (which may be provided through a VLE) to student record databases and other management information systems. A key requirement for a successful MLE is that the systems within it are interoperable, that is they can share data easily between them.

> The IMS, www.imsglobal.org/, has become the de facto standard in the area of learning technology; the framework covers specifications for metadata, content packaging, sequencing, etc. For more information about learning technology standards, take a look at the CETIS website, www.cetis.ac.uk/.

CONCLUSION

This book has attempted to reduce the complexity of the internet and the facilities it offers into a manageable set, and to show the effects of the internet, which have been enormous, on libraries. Libraries and the internet both fulfil a need for information in a variety of forms, and can be seen as both competing and complementary entities. One early apocryphal description of the world wide web compared it to a library in which the books had been dumped anywhere rather than shelved and catalogued. While the printed world of information is often harked back to and somewhat fondly remembered, it is digital information and resources that users want, for their convenience and flexibility.

However, it is clear to information professionals, and perhaps slowly becoming apparent to everyone else, that the internet offers a lot but has deficiencies, and that libraries are the best placed institution to remedy those deficiencies. It is hoped that this book will play a role in reconciling the new, digital internet world with that of the information profession in its library-based workplace, by making clear the full potential of the internet, and how information professionals can use it to promote the cause of libraries.

REFERENCES

Berube, L. (2004) Collaborative Digital Reference: an Ask a Librarian (UK) overview, *Program: electronic library and information systems*, 38 (1), 29-41.

Browning, P. (2002) *Portals and CMS: why you need them both*,

Institutional Web Management Workshop, Strathclyde.

Chowdhury, G. G. (2002) Digital Libraries and Reference Services: present and future, *Journal of Documentation*, 58 (3), 258–83.

Curtis, D. and Greene, A. (2004) A University-wide, Library-based Chat Service, *Reference Services Review*, 32 (3), 220–33.

Ellis, L. A. (2004) Approaches to Teaching through Digital Reference, *Reference Services Review*, 32 (2), 103–19.

Englert, B. (2003) *Portal Trends in Higher Education*, 19 February 2003, presented at EDUCAUSE Southwest Regional Conferences, www.educause.edu/ir/library/powerpoint/SWR0304.pps .

Ferguson, N. and Schmoller, S. (2004) *Personalisation in Presentation Services*, 4 August 2004, www.therightplace.plus.com/jp/index.html.

Library of Congress (2005) *American Memory*, http://lcweb2.loc.gov.ammem.

Moyo, L. M. (2004) Electronic Libraries and the Emergence of New Service Paradigms, *The Electronic Library*, 22 (3), (March), 220–30.

Museums, Libraries and Archives Council (2004) *The People's Network: evaluation summary*, www.mla.gov.uk/documents/pn_evaluation_summary.pdf.

Patterson, R. (2001) Live Virtual Reference: more work and more opportunity, *Reference Services Review*, 29 (3), (March), 204–10.

Place, E. (2005) Teaching Package for Internet Research, *Library Information Update*, 4 (1–2), (January/February), 39.

QCA (2004) *Key Skills Policy and Practice: your questions answered 2004* www.qca.org.uk/downloads/11483_ks_policy_practice.pdf.

SCONUL Advisory Group on Information Literacy (1999) *Information Skills in Higher Education: briefing paper*, www.sconul.ac.uk/activities/inf_lit/papers/Seven_pillars2.pdf.

index